Forgiving the
KILLER
while grieving Uriah

Forgiving the
KILLER
while grieving Uriah

SUSAN FREE

JESUS LOVES YOU

Susan Free

Forgiving the Killer

Trilogy Christian Publishers A Wholly Owned Subsidiary of Trinity Broadcasting Network

2442 Michelle Drive Tustin, CA 92780

Trilogy Christian Publishing/TBN and colophon are trademarks of Trinity Broadcasting Network.

For information about special discounts for bulk purchases, please contact Trilogy Christian Publishing.

Trilogy Disclaimer: The views and content expressed in this book are those of the author and may not necessarily reflect the views and doctrine of Trilogy Christian Publishing or the Trinity Broadcasting Network.

10 9 8 7 6 5 4 3 2 1

Library of Congress Cataloging-in-Publication Data is available.

ISBN: 979-8-89333-013-7

E-ISBN: 979-8-89333-014-4

Front/Back Cover: Design by Chris Fechter and Trilogy Christian Publishing

Editors: Trilogy Christian Publishing, Michelle Wittel, Donna Hay, Chris Fechter, and Kristy Lane

Most names in this book have been changed to protect the innocent.

Dedication

I dedicate this book to all the parents,
grandparents, and family members,
who are grieving and mourning the loss of a child.

For those of you who lost a child at the hands of another,
we pray you find strength, comfort, and
peace through the powerful act of forgiveness.

I dedicate this book to Johnny and Debbie
McDaniel, as a gift from God. You followed His
guidance to love and forgive. Thank you for sharing
your heartfelt story with us.

The Lord *is close to the brokenhearted; he rescues those
whose spirits are crushed.*

Psalm 34:18

Acknowledgments

I thank God. I thank Jesus. And I thank the Holy Spirit. Without them, I am only a shell of a person. Every night of writing was started with a prayer asking God to give me the words to write for this book. As I wrote, I felt the presence of the Holy Spirit guiding me each step of the way. I am grateful.

This book wouldn't be possible without Johnny and Debbie McDaniel's willingness to share their internal struggle of grieving their son's death, while they forgave the killer. Thank you for trusting me with your intense emotions by allowing me into your hearts. The eight-month journey of interviews will be forever etched into this book for the benefit of others grieving and needing forgiveness.

My lifetime friend Donna Hay Kelly was my greatest encourager, propping me up when I grew anxious or weary. Her daily phone calls kept me motivated to follow Jesus. My daughter, Michelle Wittel, with her calming effect, always gave me positive reinforcement. Her attention to the story line and enhancing the flow of the story made this a better book.

And with God's love, I want to thank my husband, Robert Free, for loving me and giving up our shared time together as I spent endless hours on the laptop keyboard. Thank you for supporting and understanding my desire to follow Jesus. I love you!

I want to offer a special thanks to our lead pastor

and associate pastor, after their own tragic loss, for their "profound" sermons on what it means to suffer and grieve. They inspire us to trust Jesus and keep Him close as we struggle through the trials of life.

Special thanks to my friend Chris Fechter for her graphic-artist skills in designing the book cover. Editors and friends Jerry and Donna Kelly, Scott and Michelle Wittel, Mike and Belinda West, Kristy Lane, Chris Fechter, and Sharon Weldin . . . thank you for your support as you smoothed over the words, quotes, punctuation, and tenses.

Thank you to the staff of Trilogy Christian Publishing for all your work in helping produce this book to the point of publication. You have taught me how to be a better writer through each production step. Your vision of expanding the Kingdom is serving our God in the highest. Also, thank you to my friend Carolyn Mitchell for recommending Trilogy Christian Publishing.

Table of Contents

Introduction

Our individual lives are so fragile. The house we live in could burn down tomorrow. A car accident could result in permanent injury to our bodies. Our savings account might suddenly disappear due to medical expenses. Our lives can fall apart, when we receive that one simple phone call that our child or loved one has unexpectedly died.

With just one simple phone call—life as you have known it comes crashing down. Coping with the news of losing a child or a loved one to illness, an accident, suicide, abuse, or—God forbid—a murder is extremely shocking to the heart. This shock, followed by the pain of intense grief and suffering, are difficult to manage as the heart struggles to deal with the extreme pain. This pain is indescribable and deep within.

This intense grief is the cost of loving someone. Grief is not an enemy or a sign of weakness. It is a sign of being human and loving another.[1] Grief eventually comes to everyone in life, so why do some people seem to work through it better than others? Depending on the circumstances, there is no easy answer, as everyone grieves differently. There is no right or wrong way to grieve. You have just lost someone dear to your heart. Losing a young child is particularly painful in so many different ways.

How does one deal with this all-consuming pain? Unfortunately, some will turn to alcohol or drugs to block out the unbearable pain. Others will make themselves sick with disease, unable to handle the stress. It can feel like a knife has been stabbed into your heart and you are watching yourself slowly die. You may ask, "Has God forgotten about us?" "Why is this happening, God?" Right now, it may feel like the pain may never go away; you are hurting. But there is hope and another way of surviving and living through such grief.

My name is Susan Free, and this book is based on the true story of Johnny and Debbie McDaniel and their eight-year struggle through pain, anger, and resentment after they lost their only son, Uriah, to a senseless murder. How does life go on when you struggle through the heartbreak of losing a son and at the same time, want revenge on the killer? The emotions are high! The emotions can seem out of control!

Through the McDaniel story, you will journey through their story of suffering, restoration, salvation, and forgiveness at the highest level. Yes—forgiveness for the murderer of their son. Only through Jesus' love did they learn how to love, offer forgiveness, and live and laugh again. Was it easy? Absolutely not! But it was well worth the journey to have a heart of peace once again.

When you first see the word *forgiveness*, you may think of the time when your husband forgot your birthday; or how a trusted friend didn't pay you back for the money you loaned her; or perhaps how someone told a lie about you. You may harbor deep anger or resentment for an ex-wife who divorced you; or an ex-husband who betrayed and cheated on you; or possibly parents who hurt you by physically, mentally, or sexually abusing you.

There are hundreds upon hundreds of reasons why people refuse to forgive someone for something that hurt them. All these reasons and more are hurtful events that changed your life, and each represents a significant betrayal. The thought of offering "forgiveness" is a loaded word for most people who are still wrestling and hanging on to all the emotional wounds. Each of us needs to forgive someone. How do we reach deep inside and learn to forgive those who have hurt us?

We read in Scripture, "If you forgive those who sin against you, your heavenly Father will forgive you. But if you refuse to forgive others, your Father will not forgive your sins" (Matthew 6:14–15).

When the unthinkable happened to Johnny and Debbie, their hearts were not only shattered, but they also had to cope with the emptiness, anger, and rage of knowing that the killer, during a two-minute period of uncontrolled anger, chose to take a knife and end their son's life.

This murderous act is beyond the ability to reason, so grossly unfair, so underhanded, and deceitfully wrong. The rage boils, the heart breaks, as they desperately search for some sort of uncanny justice that could level the playing field for their loss.

This book is designed to help you release the dark pain of where you are today and slowly bring you back to the land of the living, where you can find peace and acceptance and start living again.

As a writer, I thank God and the McDaniel family for their willingness to relive their eight-year struggle as they grieved the loss of their only son. I also thank them for showing us the true meaning of forgiveness, by eventually forgiving the killer during a prison visit. During our eight months of interviews, we cried many tears, we grieved in silence unable to speak, and we thanked God for the blessings of sharing this story. If it helps one person or one family with their personal struggle of loss, then all of this was worth it.

The McDaniel family sincerely thanks God for the words, for the strength, and for the comfort He offered as they recounted and relived this horrible time in their lives. Through it all, and only with God's help, can they now live a meaningful and peaceful life.

Our sincere hope is that you and your family will find some level of peace with your loss and come to a place of complete forgiveness for the person or incident that changed your life forever. Forgiveness "frees" the prisoner within you. May God bless you all.

Susan Free, writer

Johnny and Debbie McDaniel

Debbie's Prayer: "In Loving Memory"

In Loving Memory of
Uriah Ulysses McDaniel
November 18, 1976–September 10, 1997
God bless you, Uriah. See you at the house!

We begin this book with a prayer
written by Debbie McDaniel.

Dear Lord,

We come to You through Your loving Son, Jesus Christ, our Savior, and we ask You to direct and guide us as we relive the past chapters of our lives. For each person who reads this book, our prayer is that they may embark on a new journey, one in which they learn it is possible to forgive everyone and everything, including themselves.

Lord, we pray that as we record our past life experiences, we may honor our son, Uriah, who came into this world, lived for twenty years, laid down his life for another, and continues to make a difference in the world. We ask for Your grace, Lord. Grant us the strength and courage to complete this book, for we know there will be many painful moments.

Lord, truly You have shown us that "though weeping may last for a night, joy comes in the morning," and even if that morning takes years to dawn—it has been worth it. May this book be an offering of thanksgiving for Your loving-kindness and mercy. Lord, thank You for staying with us every step of the way.

Lord, take extra-good care of Uriah in Your house; stay close to Joshua, who is in prison; and mend all whose lives have been shattered by violence, bitterness, or a lack of love. May they come to know Your love, in Jesus' name we pray.

Amen.

Chapter 1

Shattered

The death of a child of any age is truly devastating. Whether at birth, from an illness, an accident, suicide, or a murder, losing a child takes an emotional toll on families.

For some families, it is the unexpected phone call in which you learn that your child has died, and from that one simple phone call comes all the anguish, pain, and suffering. Your life seems out of control. There are no words to describe how each parent or family member feels at the exact moment of hearing such horrendous news. Having a child die is one of the most painful experiences that a parent or family member will encounter during their lifetime, and for those who lose their 'only' child, the grief is compounded.

The pain and grief can be further compounded when the death comes at the hands of another human being. Parents and family members try to make sense of the inconceivable horror that someone knowingly, willingly, and/or deliberately killed their child.

There are no humanly appropriate words to soften the shocking news. The shock permeates the body in waves of unbelief and dreadful pain. Parents have described the pain as something they didn't think was possible—a pain where they can't breathe; a stabbing pain so deep it shakes the core of being alive; a dense fog that won't lift. We are in a terrible storm where our emotions are tossed around without an anchor to ground us.

Losing a child reflects back on the innocence of your child, the one you conceived and gave birth to, the one you nurtured, the one you watched walk for the first time, the one you heard say the sweet words of "dada" and "mama," and the one you adored and loved with all your heart. Now they are gone! Parents and families who lose a child experience pain that is insurmountable. There are no words to console your *shattered* hearts.

As one parent stated who lost their son to murder, "My grief was complicated by the fact that another human being chose to take my child's life. Letting the word *murder* become part of my vocabulary seemed so foreign to my tongue. Not only is my child gone, but he was murdered! It feels unreal and surreal. How can this be? This stuff happens on TV or in movies, but not in my own life, not in my home, and definitely not to my child. This news becomes a real and dark nightmare that affects everything in my life."

He goes on to say, "If I could only go to sleep and wake up to find out it wasn't true. But sleep doesn't come. My mind can't shut off as I continue to visualize the horror, over and over in my mind, of what my child must have gone through. My mind cringes over and over at the thought, unable to sleep and unable to find a way out of this nightmare. Outside, the world is still turning. Life as I knew it has just changed forever."

Families working through the issues of losing a child deserve absolute compassion and a caring heart from everyone they encounter. As one parent describes, "Losing my child for forever seems like a long time, and right now the future looks empty. Lord, teach me to embrace my grief and not fight it, so I may experience the true healing that comes from only You. My heart yearns for yesterday, yearns to do things over, and yearns for my child."

Most importantly, even though countless people have experienced their own grief, it is important to know that your path of grief will be uniquely your own. Your personal response to grief is different, and you may feel it is useless to talk to others because no one truly understands what you are going through. This is true—no one knows exactly how you feel or the depths of your pain. Yet others who have been through your type of loss may offer some support.

Go easy on yourself and take one day at a time. Patience and encouragement is needed to go through the grieving process. Surround yourself with others who have lost a loved one, if it is possible. Surround yourself with family and friends. They may not know exactly how you feel, and they may even say the wrong things at times, but they are there because they love you. Your way of grieving is unique only to you; the relationship you had with your child is only unique to you. You will grieve and mourn according to your feelings, and that is normal.

One of my grieving clients once said, "My wife died after thirty-two years of marriage, and I left the funeral early. I just wanted to go to the auto junk yard and walk around. I could no longer handle all the energy and words of the people there, so I left and found some solitude in the junk yard, where I could cry and be alone with my grief. My sorrow overwhelmed me, but the quiet, broken-down cars gave me comfort. They, too, were broken, just like me. My family ridiculed and put me down for leaving early, but it didn't matter. I had to grieve in my own way."

The grieving process generally takes longer than you can imagine. Some people try to rush this process. You never "get over" your loss, as you will always remember your loved one, but instead, you learn in time to heal as you walk "through" it. Remember, what you are feeling is not normal, but it is necessary. Knowing the Lord and His comfort does not take away the ache; instead He supports you in the middle of your ache.

Parents who lose a child to murder have many unique issues that complicate the grieving process. For the parents and family left behind, they are faced with some of the following issues that need attention, sometimes taking them away from the grieving process. Some of these include:[2]

· Lack of information about who killed your loved one and why. Are they still out there, and will they come back to hurt us?

- Endless grief and a loss of ability to work, be at home, or go to school.

- Memories or pictures of a mutilated body at the morgue. Did my loved one suffer?

- Feelings of guilt for not protecting the child. Fathers bear an unnecessary burden in our society, feeling their special role is one of protector. They suffer in silence with this pain.

- Coping with a society that blames the victim for being in the wrong place.

- Strain on marriages and family relationships.

- Effects on health, faith, and values.

- Financial burden of medical and funeral expenses.

- Finding the murderer, gathering evidence, interviews, and trial.

- Delays in a criminal trial and appeals.

- Unanswered questions of "What happened?"

As you can see from this list, the problems of survivors can seem endless. It is important to get as much help as you can to maneuver through the system as you grieve your loss. You can't do it alone. Stand with others who have suffered a loss, too. The website of the group Parents of Murdered Children has a wealth of information that can assist you.[3]

Unfortunately, across America today there are millions of hearts that have been "shattered" by the murderous death of a dad, mom, son, daughter, brother, sister, friend, and unfortunately, innocent children. Murder—a senseless death that didn't have to happen. We ask why, but we have no answers. Parents and families are left to pick up the pieces that will haunt them for the rest of their lives.

It is hard to imagine that in addition to thousands being murdered each year, there are approximately 2,300 children who go missing every day in the United States. Children can become missing for many reasons, such as misunderstandings; becoming runaways, lost, stranded, or injured; family abductions, and stranger abductions.[4] Tragically, some of these children are never found. The parents of missing children carry the additional burden of never knowing what happened to their child. The grief and pain for these families is life-shattering.

Unfortunately, crime is one thing that will always be present in society. The nature of the human mind, shaped by its childhood and life experiences, can end up in lifestyles where they are exposed to crime or exposed to parents who are violent.

The number-one reason for America's high criminal rate is the breakdown of the family. Other factors include poverty, drugs, alcohol, racism, peer pressure, parental neglect, religion, family violence, unemployment, and a general attitude toward lawlessness.[5] A breakdown in family moral values and the ease of obtaining drugs and alcohol can lead people down the road of crime.

With this trend toward violence, thousands of young victims are losing their lives, resulting in parents, family members, and friends suffering from broken hearts. This kind of unexpected and staggering loss can absolutely "shatter" the heart.

The purpose of this book is to share the eight-year struggle that Johnny and Debbie McDaniel endured after the loss of their son, Uriah Ulysses McDaniel. His twenty-year life ended when another man took Uriah's life into his own hands and murdered him due to a senseless act of jealousy. Johnny and Debbie endured pain that set them off on a trail of anger, depression, suicidal thoughts, and survivor's guilt. At times, they wanted life to end and for the pain to stop.

Gradually, they discovered other parents of murdered children who identified with their suffering. They attended private counseling sessions and healing conferences. Eventually, they learned through healing and forgiveness workshops, which included God's Word, how to minister to others to help them through the process. Their travels took them to prisons to help prisoners with forgiveness. They learned that true forgiveness is only possible through the healing strength of God.

If you have recently lost a loved one, you may not be ready for forgiveness yet, and you may not be ready for God, either—and that is a normal reaction. It may not be just about forgiving the killer; there may be forgiveness needed for the person who caused the accident; forgiveness for a person who took his or her own life; and forgiveness for yourself if you carry guilty feelings or self-blaming thoughts. You may be in the "raw" time of mourning when it is difficult to think of anything but your grief and your feelings of revenge, anger, or depression. It is normal to have those types of feelings during the grieving process. Yet there is hope available to help set you free from the pain and anguish.

Every loss has its unique circumstances that affect those loved ones left behind. Parents, grandparents, and family members who lose a child—whether from an illness, an accident, or a homicide—need extra comfort, sensitivity, and love to help them through the grieving process. The taking of an innocent life before its time is especially difficult and hard to understand.

Be encouraged that regardless of how your grief appears to you or others, it has a precious uniqueness to the One who created you. God knows intimately your personality, your relationships, and the experiences of your life. He knows your grief and isn't shocked or surprised by your responses.

Even though your heart is breaking, even though tears are filling your eyes and staining your cheeks, God does give you something worth trusting during difficult times—and that is Him and Him alone.

In your grief, may God offer you mercy, comfort, and encouragement as you read this book and search for the peace within as you begin to heal your **shattered** heart.

Jesus wept.

John 11:35 NKJV

Chapter 2

Our Life with Uriah

Hello . . . my name is Johnny McDaniel, and my wife, Debbie, and I lost our son, Uriah Ulysses McDaniel, to a violent, murderous, senseless act that ended his young twenty-year life, and this dramatically changed our world forever. Even though Debbie was Uriah's stepmother, she had become the mother figure in his life for the last ten years of his life. They were very close, and Debbie loved him like he was her own son with a motherly love that he cherished.

Our hope is that you won't judge us too harshly for all the crazy choices we made in our young-adult lives. We were typical young people with little direction in life, and we made some poor choices that affected our lives.

Our story represents our eight-year struggle to fight off the depths of depression, addiction, suicidal thoughts, and resentful hatred toward the person who took our son from us. We went through the intense shock, anger, and depression of grief, along with the emotionally charged trial and sentencing of the murderer. We spend years in therapy and ended up teaching workshops on love and forgiveness in a prison ministry. Later on in years, we finally drummed up enough courage to meet the murderer of our son and offer true forgiveness. No, we will never forget what happened. No, he will never be our friend. Yet, through the struggle and God's unconditional love, we now live in peace, knowing we were able to forgive, walk on, and calm our hearts.

If you have lost a child to a murderer or at the hands of someone whose actions caused an accidental death, you may be in a place right now where forgiveness is not an option. The disappointment, anger, and loss can consume your everyday life. You may be beside yourself—looking for an end to the bitter, all-consuming pain. Will it ever go away? We, too, went through those same feelings. We hope our struggle and what we went through as we learned to trust God will help you find the peace you desperately need to go on living life.

Even if you don't believe God can help you right now, please read on, as there are many helpful organizations that can gently help you maneuver through all the feelings associated with grief and the difficultly of losing a child.

In 1997, Debbie and I were living in Oakland, California. Our son, Uriah, who had left home at the age of nineteen, was staying with friends, three hours east of Oakland, in a small town called Placerville, near the Sacramento Valley. His birth mom, Susie, also lived in Placerville, and even though she had been primarily out of his life when he was between nine and nineteen years old, he still had a yearning to connect with her.

Uriah's birth mom, Susie, and I had had a young, rocky marriage, and we divorced when he was only two years old. We were young—twenty and nineteen years old—and we both drank alcohol and used some drugs, while managing to maintain jobs and a home. After our divorce, Uriah grew up being transported back and forth between two unstable households. This must have been very stressful for him. I know it was stressful for all of us. Being a single parent, Susie was overwhelmed by the responsibilities of juggling care for Uriah, maintaining a job, and keeping up with household chores. I was stressed by not having my family together and not seeing Uriah except on weekends and during the summers.

I am sure our stress created a chaotic living situation for Uriah. As the drug use increased, Susie took Uriah at age three and moved around frequently. At times it was hard to track her down. At one point, she quietly moved out of state, and I didn't get to see Uriah for months at a time. I became anxious not knowing where she lived and being unable to find my son.

Susie eventually moved back to California, to Placerville, where she enrolled Uriah in school. When he was between six and nine years old, she had him changing schools up to five times a year. Her life was in chaos, and she couldn't seem to stay in one place more than a few months before she longed for the next one. I had him on weekends and for most of the summers. The chaos, the unstable living environment, and the insecurity created a real struggle for Uriah.

It hurts me to think back on how he was shuffled from home to home, from school to school, and how he was exposed to all kinds of environments that are not good for kids, all without having a secure place to call home. I felt guilty that I couldn't be with him all the time and protect him from the lifestyle he was exposed to every day. I wanted custody of him full-time to take him away from all the dysfunction. I didn't know what to do.

When Uriah was nine years old, Susie ran off with a boyfriend, leaving Uriah all alone. She didn't call me to come and get him; she just left him to take care of himself. She couldn't handle the hectic lifestyle of raising a child while being a single mom, and of course, her cocaine use didn't help. To this day, we are not sure how long Uriah was left alone homeless before the police found him.

The police picked up Uriah wandering the streets and put him in a detention facility for kids to keep him safe. The court system sent a letter to my mom's address instead of my address, stating that if I wanted custody I needed to show up in court on a particular date or Uriah would be turned over to foster care. I had just happened to visit my mom the day before, and she handed me this unopened letter. When I read the letter, I was shocked that the court date was scheduled for the very next morning, three hours away in Placerville.

I frantically drove to Placerville and showed up at the court the next morning. I sat quietly and anxiously waited for court to begin. I cried as I watched little Uriah, through the window, all alone in the detention room. He couldn't see through the one-way window. When they brought him out to sit on the chair, the judge asked the courtroom, "Is there one of Uriah's parents here in the room who would like to claim custody?" I answered with a booming voice, "Yes, I am his dad, and I would love custody of my son." When Uriah looked up and saw me, the biggest smile broke across his face. He was so glad to see me, and I was so glad to see him. I loved him with all my heart. It was one of those "God moments," and I was so thankful I had gotten the letter in time to appear in court. Otherwise, he would have been placed in foster care. The judge smiled when he saw how little Uriah reacted to me when I spoke up. I was given full custody the very same day by the judge and was allowed to take Uriah home with me. I was so thankful and so happy to have my son back in my care.

It took some adjustment learning to be a full-time dad, but we loved being together. I took him swimming at the lake, and we loved playing baseball together. Other times, we just hung out, creating a routine that worked for both of us. I had close friends who watched over him after school while I worked.

I noticed shortly after we started living together that Uriah would sneak some alcohol off into his room and drink with some of his friends. I had alcohol around and drank a couple of beers after work with my friends, but I didn't think too much of it at the time. This is an example where dads need to be aware that what we do "models" behavior for our kids. Uriah watched me enjoy my beers, and he wanted to be just like his dad. I still used some drugs, but I didn't use any in front of my son. Regardless, our children are very observant and notice our behaviors.

As parents, we don't realize the impact that our behaviors have on our children. Thinking back, I feel guilty knowing Uriah went through so much. I don't know what he was exposed to from the ages of three to nine with his birth mom's lifestyle. I truly wish I could have done something to get custody of him sooner.

When Debbie, his stepmom, and I eventually met and married, Uriah was ten years old. We created a safe and stable home for him. We didn't move or have him change schools, so he finally began to thrive and feel more secure. He slowly opened up, especially to Debbie, talking more about life, knowing he had a safe family. We observed him gradually becoming calmer and more peaceful.

Debbie ponders in her quietness and says, "Uriah was such a blessing to me. I had always wanted a son. I knew I probably couldn't conceive and have children, so Uriah was very important to me. When I met Johnny, I observed that Uriah had some anxious tendencies, and my heart went out to him. I spent time with him by playing games, building LEGO projects, and talking to him about school, homework, and his friends. He responded with a gentleness and calmness that revealed his trust in me. One of my favorite things to do was read to him. He loved hearing stories about the Bible, and we spent hours talking about Jesus and His love for us."

Johnny smiles as he reflects, "He loved to play his guitar, playing all types of music. He would play for six hours at a time in his room. Our friends considered him to be a natural musician with the gift of playing his electric guitar and then jumping to the piano to play the same song. Even though he had never learned to play the piano, he had a natural gift of hearing the music and being able to write and play it."

When Uriah was a teenager, he loved to write songs, and he even had the opportunity to sell one of his songs to the musical group Pegasus, but he refused because he wanted to keep it as one of his first written songs. Friends would say he had the gift of being the next Carlos Santana or Eric Clapton. We were always amazed at his ability.

As a teenager, being smaller than most of his friends, he took up judo, a Japanese martial-arts defense program. He became pretty confident and proud that he could handle or defend himself in a dangerous situation.

Unfortunately, as do many typical teenagers, he loved to drink beer, go to parties, and hang out with his friends. Like I mentioned before, he probably watched me during his growing-up years and thought, *If Dad does it, it is okay. I want to be just like my dad.* As I look back, I sincerely wish I could have eliminated alcohol and drug use from my life before his teenage years. When we are in the middle of alcohol and drugs, we have the false feeling that no one else notices our addictions. We learn to tell ourselves lies so we can hide behind our addiction.

I myself grew up without a dad; I never knew him, and I have never met him to this day. He left my mom with three young boys and headed for greener pastures. We heard later that he was in jail, but we never learned why. I grew up feeling sad and angry that my dad would just walk off and never want to see his boys again.

Not having a dad was hard, especially since my older brother used to beat on me every day in a cruel way. I lived in fear every day of my life. I am not sure if he was angry because Dad was gone, but he took it all out on me. He would get me down on the floor and sit on me, slapping me until I quit breathing. Sometimes he would choke me until I passed out. I am not sure how, but I always regained consciousness. I truly believe to this day that God was watching over me, because no one else in the family did anything about it. Mom just thought we were two brothers wrestling around, and no one defended me as I struggled to fight him off.

One night after dinner, I got up from the table to take my plate to the kitchen sink, and my brother jumped up, came in the kitchen, and drop-kicked me in the stomach. It scared me to death. I fell to the floor and started vomiting. Even in school, he would pick fights with me in the locker room. The teacher and principal would both comment, "Why do these two have to fight at school? Why don't they just take it home to fight it out?"

I will never forget the time my brother took me and my new puppy up on the second-level balcony of our house, and then he laughed as he shoved the puppy off the porch to his death below. I watched as my puppy hit the ground below, not having a chance to survive such a fall. I was mortified and so terrified of my brother.

It is a wonder I survived my childhood. The pressure was so great at times that I would beg my mom to let me go stay with my grandma each summer. It was the only time in my childhood when I had some semblance of peace. Otherwise, I lived in constant fear. I grew up feeling so anxious. As I look back, I know God was with me to protect me. He had a plan for me, but I didn't know it then. I was just scared to death of my brother. I hid or ran from him whenever I saw him coming, because I knew he was going to try to hurt me.

In school, I eventually trained as a wrestler to learn some moves on how to defend myself. I also learned to run—and I mean *run*—as fast as I could to get away from my brother. When I would see him coming, I would take off sprinting as fast as I could go to get away or hide from him. I was terrified! Through the chaos, I eventually became a gifted runner in high school, setting track records in 1972–1974. People didn't realize I learned to run so fast to avoid abuse from my brother.

My mom didn't see the devastation I was experiencing on a day-to-day basis. As a teenager, I eventually turned to drugs to escape the mental agony. I started off with smoking pot, thinking I wouldn't progress into harder drugs, but I did. I buried my pain with cocaine for a number of years.

Unfortunately, when I married and had my son, I didn't realize the impact of my addictive behaviors and how they affected my son. Parents model behaviors for their kids to follow. Children love their parents and want to be just like them. We think we are hiding our addictions from our kids, but they are watching our every move.

As I look back, I am not proud of the life I led. I classified myself as a "functional alcoholic and drug-addictive man." I held good jobs and supported my family, and I didn't think anyone noticed my addictions. I spent quality time with my son playing sports, going places, and listening to his music. We had a genuine father/son relationship that I loved. I was determined to be a good father in spite of my upbringing and my addictions. I always vowed to stay present in his life. I loved him so much.

Two years before Uriah was murdered, I tried to get off alcohol and cocaine myself, and I was even successful for two to three months, only to then relapse. I kept repeating this cycle over and over. Eventually, my wife told me that things needed to change, because my behavior was not helping our family. I was wasting extra money on alcohol and drugs when we needed it to pay bills. My focus became unbearable as I frantically tried to find the drug of choice. I was now out of control with my addiction, and Debbie urgently asked me to try a thirty-day recovery program. At this point, I was sick and tired of feeling sick and tired, and so I said, "Yes, I will try recovery." I had hit rock bottom, and I was ready to make a change in my life.

I felt so much shame having to call my boss at work and explain that I had a drug problem and needed help in a rehab program, as if he probably already didn't know. We only fool ourselves, thinking other people don't notice our addictions. When he gave me his full support, I was so relieved that I wouldn't lose my job. He understood and said he would be available if I needed help in any way. My boss gave me the respect I desperately needed under the circumstances.

When Debbie and I went to the recovery program to enroll, we found out we didn't have enough money for me to enroll in the program, so she suggested NA (Narcotics Anonymous[6]). NA is a nonprofit fellowship or society of men and women for whom drugs have become a major problem. Recovering addicts meet regularly to help each other stay clean. This is a program that requires complete abstinence from all drugs. There is only one requirement for membership: the desire to stop using.

I eventually joined AA (Alcohol Anonymous[7]), too. AA is a fellowship of people who come together to solve their drinking problem. It doesn't cost anything to attend AA meetings. There are no age or education requirements to participate. Membership is open to anyone who wants to do something about their drinking problem.

I attended two regular meetings per week, and on rough days, when the desire to use alcohol or drugs returned, I am not ashamed to say I would attend four meetings per day. I wanted desperately to stay clean and sober. My life needed to change. I even volunteered to make coffee for the group for the next ninety days. A few weeks later, a newcomer needed a ride to the meetings, so I volunteered to pick him up twice a week. These commitments helped me stay dedicated to attending the meetings and gave me the pleasure of being helpful.

I learned that we can't get clean doing this alone. We need other people who have been through the same addictions. We need to help support one another and hold each other up when we feel like we want to fall back into those addictions. We come to believe that a higher power greater than ourselves can restore us to sanity.

Narcotics Anonymous asked me to speak to the group a few times each month, and I scheduled one speaking engagement for September 11, 1997.

I had been sober and drug free for one year and ten days when I lost my son. At the age of nineteen years, Uriah began drinking more and more, and we had to ask him to move out of our house in Oakland. I was trying hard to stay clean and sober and attend AA and NA meetings consistently. These two programs were saving my life, and I really depended on them for support. Uriah understood and said he would move to Placerville and live with friends. He wasn't ready to start going to meetings and change his lifestyle at that point, so he moved.

Even though he had his own drinking issue, Uriah was a gentle giant with a soul to match; he was always helping others in need. On several occasions when I would visit him, I would walk down the streets of Placerville with my son and catch him leaving pizza slices on napkins, on top of garbage cans, so the homeless people wouldn't have to dig for food. His heart was always caring for others, sensitive to their needs without judgment. I always enjoyed spending time with him. His zest and love for life was encouraging, and he always had a smile on his face.

As we look back, we realize we had messy lives, some due to our upbringing and some due to making our own poor choices. We didn't know God and His instructions for our lives. We learned some hard lessons, but through it all, there was one consistency: we always loved Uriah with all of our hearts.

The one event we weren't prepared for came as a shock to our hearts and shattered them into little pieces.

My tears flow endlessly;

they will not stop

until the LORD *looks down*

from heaven and sees.

Lamentations 3:49–50

Chapter 3

Our Tragic Day

Debbie cries quietly as she reflects back to the tragic day of Wednesday, September 10, 1997, and she says, "This is a day Johnny and I will never forget." Our morning started off normally at 6 a.m. as we got ready for work, totally unaware of what a surreal heartbreak the day would bring us later on. We both hurried around, grabbing a quick breakfast of coffee and toast as we said our goodbyes. Johnny hurried off to join the madhouse of rush-hour traffic in Oakland, knowing it would take one long hour to drive seven miles to the Bay Bridge, and then another thirty minutes to get into downtown San Francisco.

Johnny worked as a senior construction estimator for a company located just south of San Francisco. Johnny says, "My job was to draw up plans, estimates, and determine the overall costs of a new or existing construction project. I would create a list of approximately 150 line items of all the needed materials and write down the estimated amount necessary to complete the project. The responsibility of procuring new work for our construction company carried more pressure and stress than I needed; yet I still loved my job. Previously I had spent seventeen years as a commercial tradesman plasterer, where I applied plaster to interior walls, decorative molding on ceilings, and other surfaces."

Debbie softly mentions, "I took public transit to my job. I had to ride two different buses to get to the BART rail system going into downtown Oakland. It took me one hour to travel the short distance of five miles to reach my office. Traffic was a constant nightmare each day, but we had learned to accept it."

"I worked at the Central Office/Oakland for the Alcoholics Anonymous (AA) program, as an administrator, training volunteers on 'how to be calm' as we took calls on the AA hotline. I was involved in the more difficult suicidal calls where the caller sometimes had a gun to their head ready to pull the trigger." Johnny says, "No one ever did, as they listened to her calm, reassuring voice on the other end of the line. She had a gentle and caring way with people, understanding the agony of alcoholism."

When asked about her past, Debbie responded, "Yes, I had a drinking problem for about five years. I thought I could handle it because I was able to go to work each day, purchase a home, and keep my relationships intact. In actuality, I needed alcohol to hide my pain." She said sadly, "I had a big hurdle to climb over from childhood trauma, where I needed alcohol to numb the agonizing pain of being sexually abused by someone I cared about at the age of thirteen. I couldn't understand why this person, who was so loving and caring, would want to hurt me in that way."

Debbie went on to say, "To make matters worse, my mom took me to a chiropractor for back pain at the age of fourteen, and he also sexually molested me during treatments. I was able to tell my mom, and when my dad heard about it, he became very angry and went to the chiropractor's office, got the X-rays, withdrew me from the treatments, and let the doctor have a piece of his mind." It all became very confusing as I pondered, "Is this what adults do to children?" I was always taught to be respectful of adults and do as I was told, yet this abusive behavior was tearing me apart inside."

Debbie grew up the daughter of a pastor, singing in the church choir while attending weekly church activities. She comments, "Hearing the Word of God was a good start to life, and I even talked to God every day, but then as I left home, I found worldly things, such as making money, climbing the corporate ladder, and alcohol, that gave me more pleasure. I became more prideful, thinking of myself and what I could obtain and be in the world. I left God behind."

Johnny mentioned, "Debbie has a gentle heart, is soft-spoken, and is one who cares for people. She has empathy for others and understands what they go through. You could say she has the gift of mercy. Debbie had been sober for five years when we received the terrible news that changed our lives."

Around 5 p.m. on that terrible day of September 10th, Debbie and a co-worker (a woman Debbie was sponsoring in the AA program) left work to drive to Debbie's home to discuss the program. Nancy, the co-worker, had a car, so Debbie didn't have to take public transportation that night.

Debbie quietly recounts the moment of arriving at home and walking through the front door. "I didn't notice the red blinking light on the answering machine with several messages on it. As Nancy and I prepared to get comfortable in the living room, the phone abruptly rang with a loud shriek, echoing throughout the house. I decided to go ahead and answer the phone, even though I didn't normally interrupt AA-sponsored sessions."

Uriah's aunt was calling from Placerville. Aunt Serena frantically screamed into the phone, "Why haven't you picked up your messages? I have been calling all day!" She then screamed in exhaustion that "someone killed Uriah!" Serena, having been frantic all day trying to reach Johnny and Debbie, broke down and sobbed, releasing all the pent-up tension and anxiety she had stored inside herself all day. She was grief-stricken as she sobbed into the phone.

Upon hearing Serena scream into the phone that Uriah had been killed, Debbie stated, "There was this eerie silence of disbelief, and then I went absolutely NUMB. I couldn't speak, and my mind was racing as the blood drained out of my face." Debbie continued, "Even though my mind whirled with so many thoughts, I did have one main concern," and that was "How was I going to tell Johnny about his son? Would he break his sobriety and start drinking again?" She feared the worst and was so afraid he might start using cocaine again. She suddenly felt so fearful of what his reaction might be upon hearing this horrible news.

She also had a brief flash of a vision she had experienced four years ago and never told anyone except a prayer partner. She had a forewarning where God told her that someone would need to identify Uriah's body in the morgue. In the vision, she looked at Uriah's lifeless body and saw purple orbs coming out of his head and an angel figure rubbing his head saying, "Everything will be okay." This vision had startled her, and she didn't know what the purple orbs were, but right now she couldn't go there. She had to bury it in her mind and concentrate on how she was going to tell Johnny that Uriah was gone.

When she hung up the phone, she stood there in disbelief, not sure what to do next. Her mind did not want to engage, but then it came to her that contacting Johnny's NA sponsor and his best friend, Brian, might be helpful. Brian was one of those rare friends who can be very caring, friendly, and supportive. He might be able to give Johnny additional support once he heard this earth-shattering news.

But for right now, she just needed to be there for him. Johnny would be coming home from work any minute. She asked Nancy to stay with her until he got home. She was afraid to be alone. Her thoughts were racing, and she still couldn't believe what was happening. Yet the vision of God's previous warning remained with her.

Nancy quietly remained in the kitchen as she watched Debbie pace nervously around the kitchen. She could tell Debbie was mentally preparing what she was going to say when Johnny came through the door. Debbie was just hoping he would get home at his usual time and not hear the news on the way home. If he did, he would never make it home safely through the rush-hour traffic.

Fifteen long minutes later, Debbie heard Johnny's truck drive up in the driveway. She heard his driver's door slam. She felt her heart beating faster. How was she going to tell him? She instantly felt the dread of what she was about to do: tell the person she loved the worst thing he would ever hear in his life, that someone had killed Uriah.

Johnny came through the door and said, "Hi, Deb," but he stopped short when he saw the look on her face. "What is the matter, did something happen to you?"

Debbie looked down as tears streamed down her face, and then Johnny knew that something was terribly wrong. Debbie relived that awful moment: "I walked toward Johnny, took both his hands, and said, 'Someone murdered Uriah last night'." "I felt such pain as I watched his eyes bulge as he silently took in the news, and then I watched him slowly slide down the wall to the floor, crying out, 'No! No! No!'"

Johnny soberly relived this moment: "My brain went numb. I felt like a big shock wave had just hit me. What? Uriah murdered? The shock caused my mind to stop thinking as all thoughts disappeared." Debbie told me later that my eyes bulged and I went into some kind of shock, and I kept saying, "No, No, No," as I slid down the wall to the floor. "I couldn't register in my mind what she had just said. My mind seemed to be in a fog with white waves of shock, and my world stopped. Nothing made sense." I thought, *Killed? Could this really be true? Murdered? What in the world is going on?*

As I sat on the floor, my world just seemed to fall out from under me. I felt nausea move into my throat. My head was pounding, and my heart felt like it couldn't beat fast enough to keep up with the shock. Uriah was my only child, my only son, and now he was gone. Just like that—I couldn't believe this was true. How could he be here one second, one minute, one day, and then be murdered the next? There is nothing that prepares a parent for how to handle this kind of staggering news.

Debbie sat with me on the floor and told me a little more. "Uriah was murdered by someone, we don't know who or why yet. His body was found face-down in the creek." Debbie relives this moment: "It was just awful as I tried to keep it all together for Johnny, even though inside I felt completely numb. I describe it as a pain in the stomach that reaches a new low that a human can never prepare for in life."

In sadness, Johnny said, "When I pictured Uriah face-down in a cold creek, I just sank down deeper into the floor. I couldn't seem to feel anything anymore. All I could say was, 'Oh no! You're kidding me?' I was in agony, my heart felt like it was pounding out of my chest, and I couldn't catch my breath. I couldn't wrap my head around knowing my son, Uriah, was gone. He had his whole life in front of him, and now, just like that, he was gone—killed, and murdered, no less! I felt helpless and defeated. I didn't know what to do."

As Debbie helped me to stand up from the floor, my legs felt unsteady, and my hands began to shake. The devastation started to set in as I felt numb and unresponsive. Yet, I knew in my heart, I somehow had to keep putting one foot in front of the other. I needed to be there for my wife. My sweet wife, Debbie, gently mentioned that I needed to call my mom and my sister. My mind whirled with the thought, *Oh no, how are my mom and sister going to take this dreadful news?*

For some reason, the world outside did not stop to let me even soak in this horrifying news. I couldn't believe I heard the neighbor's dog barking and the kids playing in the street, yelling to each other as the skateboard went by on the sidewalk. I heard the neighbor's car drive up next door. Didn't they know my son had just been killed? Why couldn't the world stop for a minute and let me absorb this awful news? I had just lost my son—why couldn't the world stop and let me catch up?

Then my son's aunt, Serena, called again to tell us the police had asked her to come in to the coroner's office to identify Uriah's body, since we lived three hours away. More horror set in as I realized that she had to identify Uriah's murdered body. She told us that Uriah's head had been bashed in with a rock and his throat had been slit with a knife. He was left to bleed to death face-down in a cold creek.

I felt the sudden urge to go there and see his body for myself, but Debbie said, "That may not be a good idea—better to remember him as he lived and not in the horrible way he died." It was all surreal, unbelievable, and devastating. I felt slightly nauseous, not knowing what to do next. I lapsed into quietness, feeling like I was falling into a deep, dark well. No words were uttered. I couldn't speak. There were no words to describe how I felt—because I was drowning.

And then Debbie reminded me again that I needed to call my mom and sister before they found out from someone else. As she cried, she told me that we would eventually need to call the pastor for prayer and to plan for a funeral. She seemed to have enough wits about her to take the lead to organize each step. I was amazed at her strength and ability to help move me in the direction I needed to go. I just stared at her.

How did she do it? My mind was blank, and I just felt so much unspoken grief.

As I picked up the phone to call my seventy-six-year-old mom, I thought about her heart problems and wondered whether she could truly handle the news. How would I tell her that her grandson had just been murdered? She had survived coronary artery bypass surgery a few years back, but would she survive this kind of stress? Could this result in another heart attack? My mom also suffered from a neurological condition where she couldn't stop shaking. Her nervous system caused involuntary and rhythmic shaking called "essential tremors." She often shook so bad she couldn't even wear her dentures, because they just fell out of her mouth.

As the phone rang, my mom answered, and I braced myself. I found myself just spitting it out, "Mom, Uriah was murdered last night." There was silence, and then she gently spoke. "What? My goodness, what happened?" I could hear her voice tremble as she spoke. I told her we didn't have much information yet, but what we did know was that he had been found face-down in a creek with his head bashed in, and then my voice cracked and I started to cry. "Mom, his throat was slit! Oh God, Mom, this is horrible." I sensed her head was hanging down as she cried and cried. Then suddenly she spoke up that she would call my sister and ask her to drive her to my place. She ended the call by saying, "Son, I will see you in an hour."

My sister, bless her heart, heard the shocking news and went right into action. She volunteered to drive Mom to our place just as soon as they were packed. She was at a loss for words as to why anyone would want to hurt Uriah, who was so kind and caring. It still amazes me that everyone handles shocking news differently. Some people are devastated and can't function, while others jump into action to help everyone get through it.

As I hung up from the phone calls, the horror grew in my mind. I began to tremble, and then a sudden burst of anger overcame me, and I just wanted to smash something. My head was spinning, and I was unable to control all the emotions that were raging inside. Debbie reminded me, with a gentle touch on my arm, that we should call a few close friends and our pastor, not only to pray for us, but to plan a funeral. I don't remember much about those phone calls. I don't remember talking to the pastor. The whole evening was a blur. I do know the funeral was planned for the next week, on September 16, 1997.

Throughout our eight-year marriage, Debbie attended church on a regular basis. She played hundreds of old hymns on the organ and was very involved in the activities of the church. Uriah attended with her and even played his guitar from time to time for the congregation. Many times Debbie and Uriah would sit quietly on the sofa and read from the Bible. I believed that God existed, and I had faith that everything would work out for good; yet I was not following the teachings of the Lord. I didn't study the Bible or attend church except on special occasions. I am not sure why.

The next few days, I felt so numb and paralyzed, like I was just going through the motions. I was wandering around in a blurred state of mind. I was told there were about thirty people at our house during the forty-eight hours after we heard the news, but unfortunately, I don't remember much of the conversations.

Remember, I was scheduled to speak at the NA meeting on September 11, 1997, which was the day after Uriah was murdered. I kept my commitment, even though it was very difficult. Debbie and I attended the meeting, and I spoke to the group, with a cry rag in my hand. I cried out with all my pain that my son had been murdered the night before, but that I was there because I would need their help to get through the pain. I was there dedicating the rest of my life to honor God and Uriah, and to never, ever take alcohol or drugs again. Alcohol and drugs will only land you in jail, a mental institution, or the graveyard. Now my son was dead.

Life had become a blur, and the details of what happened to Uriah came in slow. Within a few days, we learned from the investigating detective that a young, fourteen-year-old girl had been with Uriah as they walked down the street, along with a male friend, called Joshua. Uriah had just met Joshua a few days before, even offering him a place to sleep at his aunt's house. But the aunt took one look at them and said to her nephew, "If you want to stay here, Uriah, you can, but your friend Joshua can't stay here. He will have to stay someplace else." She had an uneasy feeling about him from the start. Uriah, having such a caring heart, said he would leave and hang out with his friend, since Joshua didn't have a place to stay. That actually was the kind of heart Uriah had—he would never abandon a friend in need and leave them alone. Uriah had a compassionate heart, so he left his aunt's house to stay with Joshua so he wouldn't be alone. Looking back, since Uriah, at the age of nine, had been left alone as a child, he might have had empathy for Joshua because he understood what it was like to be alone and homeless.

On the night of the murder, Uriah, Joshua, and this fourteen-year-old girl attended an adult party, where drinking was pushed and permitted, even though they were underage. The party was starting to get out of hand with heavy drinking. At one point, Joshua drew out a knife as he danced with the fourteen-year-old girl, then he took the knife and lifted up her dress. This shocked Uriah, and he told the young girl that he would stay by her side to protect her, at least while Joshua was around. Joshua decided it was time to leave the party, and he asked the fourteen-year-old girl to go with him. Uriah decided to go with them, not knowing if Joshua might try to rape or otherwise hurt her. Uriah didn't know the young girl very well, but he felt she might not be safe alone with Joshua.

The young girl later shared with the police that they had been drinking. They laughed and carried on about every silly thing as they walked down the street. Uriah and the girl were laughing and being flirtatious, even locking arms at times as they walked. The young girl noticed that Joshua was becoming a little agitated as he glanced over at them with a scowl on his face. It appeared he was jealous of the attention Uriah was giving the girl.

All of a sudden, as they arrived at the corner of the bridge crossing the creek, Joshua motioned to Uriah to come with him. Uriah followed him into the thick brush down to the creek. The fourteen-year-old girl stayed up at the corner of the bridge, not knowing for sure what was happening. But then the girl heard Uriah say in a loud voice, "No, Joshua, don't do it!"

and then she heard a loud crunch. Most likely, this was when Uriah was hit in the head with a large rock. Joshua came out of the brush with blood on him and said to her, "Let's get going." She asked, "Where is Uriah? Isn't he coming with us?" But Joshua silently took her arm and hurried off toward town. She remained silent as they walked. She had the sick feeling that something horrible had happened back at the bridge, and fear washed over her as she visualized herself as the next victim. She decided to be quiet and not ask any further questions.

As Debbie and I listened to all the details about our son's death, it was extremely agonizing. My thoughts went to how horrible it was that Uriah had to suffer such a terrifying death, to why would anyone would want to kill him. From there, my mind went to more disturbing thoughts such as, *I will kill the guy who did this to my son! If he thinks he can take my son's life, I can take his, too!* Nothing made sense as I fought the battle that blindly raged inside me. Deep inside me, I knew revenge was not the answer, but for what God-forbidden reason did he have the right to kill Uriah? So many questions were racing through my mind, and I had no answers. The grief was breaking our hearts.

Forgiveness is giving love when there is no reason to.

Anonymous

Chapter 4

Six Days of Trauma

The crime victim's advocate called us on the evening of September 10, 1997, the same day Uriah was murdered. He was the detective assigned to our case, and he was there to keep us informed of the investigation and help us with any questions. He shared that a knife had been found under Uriah's body as he lay dead in the creek. They felt certain this was probably the murder weapon. As parents, this was hard for us to hear, since the shocking news of his death right now was such an open, raw wound.

We were told the fourteen-year-old girl who had been with Uriah and Joshua that evening had gone to the police station. She gave her statement of what she had seen and heard the night before. She identified Joshua as the one who went into the brush with Uriah. The police had started to look around Placerville for him, thinking Joshua might still be in town. An eyewitness had said they saw someone who looked like him at the scene of the crime at Hangtown Creek. The same day, on September 11, as the police were investigating, Joshua appeared as a bystander, talking to people standing around at the scene of the crime. He asked questions on what had happened, pretending he didn't have anything to do with the murder.

When we heard this, we couldn't believe he had the gall to go back to the scene. How could one person be so arrogant and self-absorbed? To think he went back to the scene of the murder and had the audacity to talk with investigators, hoping he would divert their attention from him, was incomprehensible. Research shows that some criminals return to the scene of the crime to relive the thrill, to feel powerful and invincible. Other criminals return to the scene to try to make things right, to try to undo the crime. It is all about narcissism.

Later in the afternoon, the murderer must have realized things were getting too heated for him, and he decided to leave town. He went back to his place and packed his personal clothes, including a bag of the bloody clothes he'd worn when he killed Uriah. He had plans to dispose of them on his way out of town, but the sheriff pulled up right in front of his car as he was leaving and arrested him. The bag of bloody clothes offered additional important evidence that helped keep him behind bars until the trial.

Another valuable piece of evidence came to light within a few days, when another man, who had read about the murder in the newspaper, came forward and said that Joshua Smith had stabbed *him* four times on a recent trip to Los Angeles. This had happened about thirty days before, when they ran out of gas. This man said he had been arguing with Smith's girlfriend, and Smith "got angry and came over and stabbed him four times." Luckily, he lived to tell about it. Recently, while reading the newspaper at home, he had seen the headlines that Uriah McDaniel had been murdered by Joshua Smith. He recognized Joshua as his attacker and felt he needed to report the injuries he had suffered at the hands of this person. The identification of Joshua as his own attacker added more fuel to the fire to help later convict him.

No one could dispute that Joshua had a temper and had been involved in multiple violent incidents. He was now in jail, though, and we could relax a bit, knowing he was not out in the public where he could threaten or hurt us or others. It eased our mind to know he was locked up.

Looking back, I do feel we were fortunate to know who the killer was within a few days and to know he was in custody. I don't know how families survive who wait for years to find out who killed their loved one and then go through years waiting for a trial. The wait and the unknown would be so stressful on the family members. Millions of other families suffer without knowing where the body of their child is and sometimes never finding out what happened. Only Jesus can offer peace to those suffering families.

The one question that went around and around in my head that I needed to ask the detective was this: "Did my son suffer very long?" With his throat being slit, I hoped and prayed that he hadn't suffered very long. The detective responded, "In my years as a detective, I have learned that someone having this type of injury probably doesn't live more than a minute or a minute and a half. They may even be unconscious during that entire time." When I heard this, I lost control of all my emotions and let go with deep, heart-wrenching sobs. The detective reached out to me in empathy, put his arms around me, and just held me. I hurt so much from the pain of knowing

Uriah had died such a gruesome death.

The six days after Uriah's murder were long. We talked to our pastor, who helped us plan a funeral—more of a celebration of his short life. We went to the funeral home to pick out a casket, and our brains were in such a fog. Trying to pick out a casket is like shopping for a new car on a big parking lot. You don't know what you want, which ones are weatherproof, which one Uriah would like, or even what the price is; you are just numb. Finally, you just point to one because the lining is Uriah's favorite color. You can picture him being protected in this soft color and design. Nothing makes sense as you make the arrangements in a brain fog. Family members need to be aware that parents need help during this emotional time, as it is very easy to overspend due to the high emotions.

In the end, due to the high cost, we decided on cremation. Before his body was cremated, we put a little iron Great Dane dog figurine in his hand. Uriah had loved his dog, Bubba. The funeral was scheduled for September 16, 1997, six days after Uriah died.

We had family and friends by our side the entire time, which helped us not fall apart completely. When your heart hurts so bad, it is difficult to sleep, eat, or visit, but I will say that the love and support of family and friends is what helped us "limp" through those first few days. We needed to talk about it over and over, asking questions, "Why?" "Why Uriah?" We didn't understand the why. Most of us think this sort of tragedy happens to other people, but not to us.

Those six days before the funeral were pretty much a mental blur, our brains in a fog that would not lift.

We cried, unable to speak at times, and then we would talk endlessly about our son. Family members around us helped plan the memorial, picking out pictures and music. Sometime during that week, I managed to sit down and write a few words about Uriah. I wanted to tell everyone about Uriah, what he was really like. The church pastor warned me that it is very difficult and emotional to speak at your own child's funeral, but I wanted to with all my heart. I wanted everyone to know what Uriah was really like and what a special son he was to us.

*Search for the L*ORD *and for his strength; continually seek him.*

1 Chronicles 16:11

Chapter 5

Saying Goodbye

There were about three hundred friends, family members, and acquaintances packed into the church on September 16, 1997, as they joined together to celebrate the twenty years that Uriah had lived. The day had come to say goodbye.

The pastor opened in prayer and then gently started talking about Uriah Ulysses McDaniel being born on November 18, 1976, and passing away on September 10, 1997. He was born to Johnny and Susie McDaniel at the young ages of twenty and nineteen years respectively. They had dated as high school sweethearts. As the pastor's gentle voice went on about Uriah's love for life, his love for his music, and his love for his friends, I found myself drifting back with thoughts to that time in high school.

I loved Susie for most of my high school years. Despite a turbulent relationship, we managed to stay together through some crazy times. We had some really good times, which included indulging in some alcohol and drugs. It was quite a shock to both of us when, after one time of being sexually active, Susie became pregnant. She was only fifteen years old. She was not ready to be a parent, and neither was I, so she had an abortion. At the time, I didn't have any concrete values as to whether it was right or wrong;

we were just too young to be parents. It was a tough time for Susie, but I stayed by her side.

Four years later, after high school, Susie became pregnant again. You would think we would have learned our lesson the first time. This time we agreed to marry, to do the right thing and have the baby. We were just kids trying to find our way. Her mom lived with us in the beginning, and as newlyweds who needed privacy, this definitely turned out to be a bad idea. I had no training, as a twenty-year-old, on how to handle a marriage, let alone a mother-in-law living with us, too.

I did have a pretty good-paying job in construction, so we rented a nice three-bedroom home, and Susie loved cooking great meals and keeping the house super-clean. I worked and felt like I finally had the family life I had yearned for all those years.

Susie wanted to have a home birth, and she managed to pull it off. Surrounded by two midwives and eight family members, she gave birth to little Uriah after seven hours of labor. Even though we were young, we were proud parents and welcomed this little guy. Unfortunately, as life progressed, our marriage relationship started a downward spiral.

We were both drinking some alcohol and using some drugs, and I decided I could sell some pot to make a little extra money to make our life better. Not a good idea, but it was very alluring to make extra money. Again, God protected me because I was never caught or arrested. I was just an immature kid.

In our early twenties, we found ourselves living

the high life with good-paying jobs, a new and bigger rental home, and a new car, and I felt like I had finally found the family life I had always dreamed of having when I was younger. Everything was going well—until cocaine entered our marriage, and our life together went straight downhill.

Susie decided to take some time and go visit some cousins for a few days. I thought how nice it was that she stayed in touch with her cousins . . . no harm in that. When she came home, I noticed something was different about her. After asking her a few questions, she said she had been unfaithful. I was furious, upset, and hurt. My world was upside down. Yet I knew I didn't want to lose her. We talked it out at length and finally agreed that our marriage was worth saving, especially since we had a son. We found working through this hurt very challenging.

Unfortunately, shortly thereafter she decided to take Uriah, our two-year-old son, with her, and she left—this time for an undetermined amount of time. I was in such pain knowing that she had left again and taken Uriah with her. I felt horrible, I felt alone, and my life was so out of control. I went to stay with my mom for a couple of weeks to avoid the loneliness. My mom talked to me every day, giving me some comfort from the nightmare I was facing.

Then I got a call from a hospital representative that my son, Uriah, was a patient in the hospital and had been removed from my wife's custody. I couldn't believe what I was hearing. Uriah was in protective custody? What was going on? I quickly learned that a male friend of Susie's had knocked his little chin through his teeth, resulting in six stitches. I couldn't believe a grown man would hurt an innocent child—especially *my* child. I was absolutely livid and beside myself. I was in a fit of rage, and at the young age of twenty-two, I didn't know what to do or where to turn. A hospital social service worker managed to help me get a public defender to begin the long process of navigating the court system.

Luckily, in this type of situation, I learned the courts actually respond rather quickly for the protection of the child. Within a few days, the courts heard my case, and since we were in a chaotic situation, the judge decided to grant my mom temporary custody until the situation could be investigated. Since I was not involved in Uriah's injuries, I could be with him at my mom's home. Susie was so anxious and depressed. The court instructed her to stay away from our son until the investigation could be completed.

My mom and I brought Uriah home to her house to stay until the courts finished their investigation. A week later, one night after dark, I heard some noise outside my bedroom window. When I reached the window, I could hear someone crying. I opened the window to see Susie there, weeping. She was completely heartbroken, and she sobbed that she desperately needed to see Uriah. Despite what we had been through, my heart went out to her, and I let her in. I still loved her in spite of everything we had been through. She crawled into the twin bed with Uriah and slept beside him all night. I watched them sleep, and it made me cry that all this was such a big mess. I prayed, "Oh, God, help us."

I am not sure how many days went by, but the courts finally released Uriah back into our care. Susie and I vowed to try again to keep our marriage together. We weren't together too long, though, before Susie asked me to move out. "Let's take a break," is what she said. I loved her so much, so I agreed, but I found myself becoming obsessed with her. I couldn't leave her alone. I didn't trust her, and yet I didn't want to lose her. I would sneak over to her house and stand outside at night to listen through the walls to see if she was talking to someone else. I was obsessed and so afraid of losing her again. I didn't want to lose my family.

I became very anxious and couldn't even concentrate on my job. I felt Susie pulling away, and I couldn't stop her. I had become the "fatal attraction." I was so brokenhearted. I didn't want my son to grow up without a family, without a dad full-time in his life. I didn't know what I was going to do, but I was determined to be in my son's life, no matter what it took. I felt like I might have a nervous breakdown.

Susie divorced me three months later. She told me, "If you hadn't bugged me all the time, I might have stayed with you." I felt like it was all my fault, and I blamed myself for my failed marriage. We managed to maintain a civil relationship after our divorce, and I was granted time with my son every weekend and most summers. Since I had experienced a rough childhood without a dad, I was so determined to love my son with all my heart and never abandon him. When we were together, I planned fun outings: We played ball, I took him to new places, and we just enjoyed our time together. I loved him so much.

For the next seven years I was single, working, living by myself, and living an insane lifestyle. Even though I had quality time with Uriah, which I truly enjoyed, I felt lost inside when I was by myself. The only time I felt happy was when I had time with my son. From the loss of my marriage and the loneliness, I drank and rebounded by dating anyone who would take an interest. I was so lonely. I felt dead inside.

God was still in my thoughts, but I certainly wasn't living a godly life at all. As I look back, I realize I didn't know God and what kind of life He wanted me to lead. I buried my pain and hurt in alcohol, drugs, and women. I became a sad specimen of a man, and I was not happy. I continued to work at my construction job as a plasterer in San Francisco, but then one day, everything changed.

I met Debbie—oh, my goodness, she stepped onto the elevator I was waiting for, and I followed. We both worked in a high-rise in downtown San Francisco. The date was April 30, 1987. She was so beautiful: blond, blue-eyed, and dressed to the nines in a gorgeous, light-blue, classy suit. She looked so good. I was in la-la land. I couldn't even talk; all I could do was stare at her. To my surprise, she just started talking to me, asking me questions. She seemed completely at ease when she asked me what floor I wanted.

I told her I was working on the thirty-second floor, the top floor of this same building on a construction site, but that other people couldn't go up there without a pass. She said, "Well, I work on the nineteenth floor, and I would like to see the top floor. Would you show me around?" Johnny thought, *Would I show her around?* My mind was racing, but I quickly recovered and said, "Absolutely, come with me, and I'll get you in with my pass." I couldn't believe I was taking her to my work site. It wasn't allowed, but I had lost sight of all rules.

I just wanted to be with her and show her around.

The other construction workers stared at her as she stepped off the elevator. They were stunned that I was with such a beautiful woman and that I was bringing her on the job site. They all knew she wasn't allowed there, but all they could do was gawk at her. No one said a word! I felt so good! I felt ten feet tall and growing, like 'Johnny the Beanstalk.'

As she got ready to get back on the elevator, I was shocked when she asked for my phone number and said, "Let's have lunch sometime?" I said, "Absolutely, I would love that, call me anytime."

The next day, I couldn't wait for her to call me. I went down to the nineteenth floor in my dirty work clothes and asked for her. She came to the reception area, surprised to see me, but she was gracious as she led me down the hall, past all the cubicles, to a corner office with a beautiful view of San Francisco. I couldn't believe my lucky stars. Who was this woman? She must be someone important to have a corner office. We had a great visit and arranged to have drinks after work. I found out later she was interviewing me by asking me lots of questions before pursuing any relationship with me. I think I passed the test, because she agreed to come to dinner at my place about a week later. I told her I would make her dinner and she could meet my son, Uriah, who was ten years old. She said, "Yes, I would love to!"

Debbie said, "I took one look at Johnny and felt feelings right off the bat. He was so handsome. When I found out he was a father to a ten-year-old son and he had a good relationship with his ex-wife, I found myself wanting to know more. I had always wanted children, but I had previously had an ectopic pregnancy at one point, and I wasn't sure I could conceive again. I had always prayed that God would give me a second chance, so knowing Johnny had a son made me happy. I was excited to get to know him and learn more about him."

Johnny clarified, "After I had asked Debbie to dinner, I realized I had just invited this professional, classy lady to my old, little ramshackle place I called home. I only paid $165 per month to rent this little place, and it was just big enough for Uriah and me to hang out in when we were together. My sister even warned me, 'Don't invite her to your home; you live in an old bachelor shack.'"

All of a sudden, I started to feel insecure, but then I thought, *If she can accept me as I am now, she can accept me as I am in the future.* I just decided to be myself and go from there.

When she arrived Friday night at 6:30 p.m., I made my favorite recipe of American goulash: a quick meal made from ground beef, tomato sauce, herbs, and elbow macaroni noodles. It was about the only thing I knew how to fix. She walked in and said hello to me, then immediately headed toward my son, who was on the floor playing with LEGOs, and she sat down with him to play. I was a bit astonished, but also very pleased that she took an interest in my son. She was so kind and gentle, and I loved it that she was playing with Uriah in such a caring way.

Debbie states, "We had dinner, talked for hours, and both played with Uriah. It was so pleasant spending time like a real family. The best part was that Uriah seemed to be very relaxed around me. He was so cute and talked to me as he played with his LEGOs." Johnny shared, "He had been part of a chaotic life for years, so it was refreshing to see him relax."

Johnny went on to mention, "For me, it had been seven long years of being single, and I was ready to marry and have a family again. When she got ready to leave, I asked Uriah what he thought of her. His response was, 'Dad, I think you should marry her.' Uriah was so cute for a ten-year-old boy to say that. He actually picked out Debbie as his stepmom."

I took Uriah at his word and married Debbie on July 2, 1989, a little more than two years after we met. I proposed to her on the porch, and we eloped to Reno to exchange wedding vows. Each year, since that first date so many years ago, we still celebrate April 30th as the beginning of our new life together. My life finally took a turn toward the "good" by meeting Debbie. God had sent me an angel.

After we were married, Debbie started attending church, taking Uriah with her every Sunday. They sang in the choir, read the Bible, and memorized verses, and he played his guitar during the offering. I hung back and didn't attend because I wasn't sure I was willing to give up my alcohol and drug use. I just wanted to work and provide for my family. Debbie was so attentive to read Scripture and other books to Uriah in their quiet time together. He began to reach out and believe in God, too. God had sent Uriah an angel.

I could tell it was important for Debbie to give Uriah a stable home life after everything he had been through. She requested his school records from the three different schools he had attended in the last year. She recognized that he had been through so much chaos that he just needed a peaceful and stable home. She helped him with his homework and spent quiet time talking to him for hours. She wanted him to begin to trust her and feel he had a safe home. Uriah seemed to thrive in this type of atmosphere. She chose to care for him with the patience and gentle love that only a mother can give, something he had seldom experienced with his birth mom. He began to trust that we were providing a safe home for him.

Johnny was jolted back to reality upon hearing the pastor finish up with his words about Uriah— and he screamed inside, "Oh no, Lord, we are at his funeral. Oh my God!" I felt the inconceivable, depressing dread permeate every cell of my body. I felt my head drop and the tears started to flow, again, this time maybe never to stop. Oh, how fast life can change. In a split second, you can lose someone you love, and life changes. My world would never be the same. Such wonderful memories I had ten years ago meeting Debbie and becoming a family unit with our son, Uriah, and now we had lost him to a senseless murder. Life just didn't seem fair. *God, oh God, why? Please help me!*

Even though I was in a difficult place with my grief, I managed to get enough of a grip to stand before everyone and give the eulogy for my son. I felt very shaky and nervous, and I was praying I could hold it together. The pastor had warned me that most family members can't get up and talk because it is so hard emotionally, but I was determined to say a few words for my son. I took a deep breath and started:

"I want to thank everyone for coming today. This means a lot to the family and really helps comfort us more than you realize. Uriah's birth mom, Susie, is here, along with Joan, Serena, Grandma, and my wife, Debbie.

"I was blessed that I had the opportunity to spend lots of time with Uriah. When he was three years old, we traveled to Oregon, just the two of us, for eight weeks. What a beautiful bonding time that was for us as father and son.

"He spent every summer with me while growing up. As a teenager, we did many things together as two buddies would do. We went swimming at the lake in Berkley, just the two of us. I used to coach him on how to talk to girls. He was really shy. I remember one time he really liked this girl at the lake. She was getting ready to leave in her car, so when we drove by in the parking lot, we drove slowly by her car, so Uriah could say something to her, but he didn't. I asked him why he didn't say anything, and he said he was too shy. I drove back around and parked by her car, and then he decided to finally say something. He just needed a little coaxing." The audience laughed at my statement.

"Uriah loved walking around downtown Berkley at night, and I would walk up and down Shattuck Street with him. He always was so kind, especially to those who didn't have much. Many times when we were walking around he would buy two pieces of pizza and give one to a homeless person. One time, he put a slice of pizza on a napkin and left it on top of a garbage can, so a homeless person would see it and not have to dig in the garbage for food.

"That was who Uriah was, always so kind. I thank God for letting me have the kind of relationship with my son that every father dreams of having in life. We were two buddies, and he even worked with me for a short time as a plasterer. He was a hard worker for his age. Uriah taught me how to live a more peaceful life. He had a tremendous amount of patience, and I remember telling myself that I wish I could be more like him.

"Uriah had a way of touching everyone's heart. He loved poetry and loved having Debbie read to him. I know he is in a better place now with his heavenly Father. Debbie taught him about Jesus, and they developed a special bond together.

"There is a scripture in 1 Corinthians 12 that talks about a variety of gifts given to us by God. One of them is the gift of faith. Even though I didn't live a godly life, I always felt things would work out for good. Uriah now lives in the House of God. Try to be happy for him. I know Uriah is there, and as believers, I know we will see him again.

"The last few days have been the worst of my life. I have been in the Narcotics Anonymous twelve-step program the last year and ten days, and last Thursday, before this tragedy happened, I was asked to be the speaker. Now his tragedy is part of my story. He will live through my heart to help other people the rest of my life.

"In the twelve-step program, we learn to take one day at a time. This means waking up and recommitting to the process every single day. This means that despite what stressful circumstances you may be facing in life, and regardless of what happened yesterday, you are making the conscious choice to carry on in your commitment to sobriety. My commitment to God and to Uriah is strong and I will stay committed.

"The last thing I want to share with you is that Uriah had the nickname 'Fingers.' He had a very gifted, special talent for music. He played the guitar and one of the songs, 'Stairway to Heaven,' was played here today. He loved to write music and would come out of his bedroom and play it immediately on the piano. He never had a piano lesson and admitted he didn't know how to play; yet he could copy any song he played on the guitar or heard on the radio, and immediately play it on the piano and sound like he was a professional. He had a rare gift.

"Thank you to all of you for being here to celebrate Uriah's short twenty-year life." At this, I felt my voice crack and the tears swell up in my eyes. My throat constricted. The pain was too great to go on . . . I felt like I could sob forever and never stop. I wanted to keep talking about him, and I didn't want to quit, but I could no longer talk. I knew that when I left the stage, I would have to say good-bye to him, and I wasn't ready. The pain was so deep-rooted, and all I could do was cry as I turned and walked off the stage.

Even though I was hurting and grieving, it did warm my heart to mingle with the three hundred guests who came to Uriah's funeral. We didn't realize so many people knew him, loved him, and wanted to support us in our grief. The love in the room felt like it was straight from God, and for the first time in a long time, I felt a stirring in me that I was so grateful for God. My life always had faith, but I did not live a godly life. At this moment, I felt a gentle nudge to turn to Him, to love Him, and to follow Him. I felt He was there in the room with me, loving me and crying with me through my grief, giving me the comfort I desperately needed.

The LORD hears his people when they call to him for help.

He rescues them from all their troubles.

Psalm 34:17

Chapter 6

Anger, Rage, and Self-Blame

As I look back, Debbie and I realized that when a death unexpectedly occurs in a family, there is the initial shock of hearts being completely shattered—and I mean, shattered into pieces. We were numb, grief-stricken, and somewhat paralyzed in our minds. Family and friends came together and rallied around us, helping us stumble through the first few weeks. As we were planning the memorial, picking out pictures and music, writing out the words to the eulogy, fixing food, and talking to family members, our hearts were breaking, but friends and family were literally holding us together.

After the funeral, we felt some contentment that perhaps we could begin to get back to a routine again. Family and friends returned to their homes to try to get back into their daily routines. They still phoned us, but not as much. As we began to think of returning to work, our world began to close in on us.

The *reality* of what had just happened began to penetrate our minds and our lives. We began to realize that Uriah, our son, would never come through the front door again. We would never hear his voice on the phone or be able to hug him again. We would never sit down to dinner or watch TV together. We began to notice the loneliness, the empty spaces, and we began to feel restless and uneasy. Debbie and I were both trying to adjust to life without him. It all began to take a bigger toll on our well-being.

We talked nonstop about Uriah, we cried, we barely ate food, and we stayed up all night talking, until finally, after we were exhausted, we fell asleep for an hour or two. This was hard on us, and as his dad, I couldn't handle the intense pain any longer. I lapsed into months of quietness where I could barely talk. I felt like I was stuck in the bottom of a dark well and couldn't get out. I didn't want to get out. I just wanted to be quiet with my grief.

Depression had reared its ugly head, but I didn't recognize it as such—I was grieving deep in my heart. Debbie went to church and found some comfort through friends, Scriptures, and sermons, but I didn't go. I wasn't ready to share my grief, and I didn't want to sit and cry in front of everyone.

One month after Uriah's funeral, we took his cremated ashes to his favorite camping spot near Cosumnes River near Placerville. There were about eight to ten family members and friends with us. We read the following poem about a child loaned, which helped us with our grief:

Child Loaned

"I'll lend you for a little time,
a child of Mine," He said.
"For you to love him while he lives,
and mourn for when he's dead.
It may be six or seven years
or twenty-two or three,

but will you, till I call him back,
take care of him for Me?
He'll bring his charms to gladden you,
and should his stay be brief,
you'll have his lively memories,
as solace for your grief."

"I cannot promise he will stay,
since all from earth return,
but there are lessons taught down there
I want this child to learn.
I've looked this wide world over
in My search for teachers true,
and from the throngs that crowd life's lanes,
I have selected you.
Now, will you give him all your love,
not think the labor vain,
nor hate Me when I come to call
and take him back again?"

Dear Lord, Thy will be done,
for all the joy Thy child shall bring,
the risk of grief we'll run.
We'll shelter him with tenderness,
we'll love him while we may,
and for the happiness we've known,
forever grateful stay,
but should the angels call for him
much sooner than we planned,
we'll brave the bitter grief that comes
and try to understand.

—Edgar A. Guest

This famous poem by Edgar Albert Guest (1881–1959) has been bringing comfort to grief-stricken parents for years. Guest himself suffered the loss of two of his children. To lose a child is one of life's most awful experiences. Focusing on the gift of your few years together can bring great comfort.[8]

As we finished the poem, tears were streaming down everyone's faces. As we took handfuls of his ashes out of the container, we noticed the little iron Great Dane dog that we had put in Uriah's hand before his cremation. It had survived the cremation process, and we were shocked. The dog was definitely scarred from the heat, but still intact. We were somewhat comforted having this little dog in our hands, feeler closer to Uriah. We then sprinkled the rest of his ashes along the trail.

A friend with a simple Instamatic camera took a picture of us, and amazingly, when she had it developed, we noticed all these purple orbs on the picture. Debbie took one look and was shocked to see the same purple orbs that she had seen in her vision four years before Uriah had died. She remembered the vision of having to identify Uriah in the morgue and the angel rubbing his head, saying, "Everything will be okay." As we were spreading the ashes, the purple orbs were all around us.

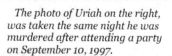

Johnny, Debbie
&
Uriah McDaniel

Uriah was ten years
old in this picture.

The photo of Uriah on the right,
was taken the same night he was
murdered after attending a party
on September 10, 1997.

The family was surprised
to see the purple orbs
floating in the picture as
they spread Uriah's ashes.
The photograph was taken
to a professional and they
said, "It was part of the
picture, not a malfunction
of the camera."

We didn't completely understand what the supernatural purple orbs meant, but we felt peaceful that they were close by, giving us comfort.

After researching the purple orbs, we found a

website by Susan Brunton that explained, "Purple is a very royal, spiritual color and can be associated with spiritual development and indicate peace and forgiveness. If you have a matter in your life that requires you to forgive somebody, you should do so and attain peace. It can also mean that you will gain wisdom. Amazingly, thousands of people have reported seeing orbs in different colors."[9]

After we finished sprinkling Uriah's ashes, we all headed home to begin life without him. Johnny mentions, "The next two years were the worst. We felt like we went through hell and back. We suffered with such intense grief. Debbie grieved quietly in her favorite chair, reading from the Bible and reflecting back on her wonderful memories with Uriah. I found myself spending more and more time being silent or quieter than normal. I buried myself in work and golf to keep busy. When I did talk, it came out in anger, rage, and self-blame.

"My friends and family would try to console me and even asked if I could forgive the murderer to help give me peace. My immediate angry response was, 'I could never, never forgive the murderer for what he did to my son. You want me to forgive that scumbag for murdering my son, slitting his throat, and crushing his skull with a rock?' No way in hell. Not ever going to happen. He killed and took my only son from me.' I was in a complete rage that some punk kid had the audacity to decide to take Uriah's life and leave us without our only child. I just wanted to smash something."

All this anger and rage was building up inside me. I even had thoughts of killing the murderer—

thoughts on how I would do it and where I would do it—and yet I knew it wasn't right. I had so many thoughts of revenge against Uriah's murderer, and I pictured myself harming him in the same way he had killed Uriah, many times over. Deep inside, I knew it wasn't the right thing to do. As sick as it sounds, I felt so guilty for not protecting my son. I started blaming myself for not being there for him. I felt guilty for what he had been exposed to in life. I felt guilty that he had been exposed to alcohol. I felt guilty about my own lifestyle. I was hurting so bad. I felt crazy inside.

All this crazy stuff inside me began to work on me, even creating suicidal thoughts. I would sometimes stand in the kitchen looking at the butcher block of knives. I would take a knife out and put it to my throat. My thoughts would go to: *All I have to do is push it in and pull it across my throat, and it will be over.* I had a need to feel what my son had gone through. I felt so much guilt, and I would have gladly taken his place so he could live. Dads are made to protect their kids, and I felt like I had failed him, so I blamed myself. Even though Uriah had lived three hours east of Oakland, I still blamed myself. The self-loathing and pain was becoming unbearable, and I felt like I could never be happy again. I really needed help to get through this grief.

I will say everyone grieves in different ways. There is no right or wrong way to grieve because it is your personal loss you have to cope with. As I look back, I might have saved myself years of anguish if I could have turned to God for help sooner, but I didn't know Him like I do now. I came to realize that God was the only way out of the hell I was going through. I saw a small sign on a counseling office bulletin board that said, "*If you are going through hell, don't stop.*" I realized I needed to keep on going until I was out of this hell.

As a married couple, we unfortunately suffered separately as we worked through our grief. The connection between a husband and wife can be the source of the greatest joy or the most intense pain in a person's life. When our spouse is going through a troublesome time, or even a season of suffering, our heart breaks along with theirs. If we can't do anything to solve the issue, it causes us great pain. Sometimes the heartache comes from the actions of our partners. They may be making poor financial decisions, experiencing bad health, or being away from home more than usual.

It is worth noting that men and women grieve differently, and this became very apparent in our marriage. I retreated deep inside myself, unable to speak or express myself in an appropriate manner. I found myself lost and just going through the motions by working on my construction job, and then on weekends, all I wanted to do was just go play golf. I wanted to get away from the pain of losing Uriah and focus on something that diverted my pain for a few hours. I would even say I became a golf junkie. I had a hard time sitting at home doing nothing, so I kept busy. When I did speak, I found myself angry and raging at matters that hurt my wife.

Debbie states, "I didn't know what to do with Johnny. He was in so much pain, and his way of coping was going to work and playing golf every chance he had free. I grieved quietly as I thought about Uriah and the special times we'd had together. I remember all the hours of spending time with Uriah as he grew up. Uriah was only ten years old when I first met him, and he seemed anxious, uncertain, but yet quiet. He had been in and out of different schools over the first five years of elementary school, and his birth mom wasn't always available to him emotionally or physically, so he desperately needed a mother figure in his life to nurture and listen to him."

Debbie went on to say, "I spent years listening to Uriah's ideas as he plotted and schemed about what he was going to do next. He was sweet, caring, and really believed in people and their value of self-worth. I helped him with homework and school projects, and I taught him about God's Word. I would read Scriptures from the Bible and teach him about God's love for us. He attended church with me and eventually played the guitar for the worship team."

Debbie remembers one episode when his two dogs went missing: "We frantically looked all over for the dogs, talked to neighbors, put up flyers offering a one-hundred-dollar reward, and started praying for their return. The next morning we prayed again, as we continued our frantic search for the dogs. During our search, Uriah ran across a Great Dane who was hungry and skinny and had been neglected. He asked if he could bring the dog home and take care of it, and I said, "Yes, since you can't find your dogs, you can keep this one,' and he ended up calling him Bubba."

We continued to pray for the return of his other two dogs and started calling the dog pounds. One small local pound said they had received a report of two dogs traveling together, and they had picked them up. We eagerly drove over to the pound to pick up two very happy, tail-wagging dogs. We laughed because now Uriah had three dogs to take care of. Debbie recalls, "Those memories of working together to find the dogs really bonded us."

During this interview, as Debbie reflects back on the wonderful memories she had with Uriah, she quietly sobs. Her grief runs deep as she talks about her love for sweet Uriah. She remembers the feelings of grieving alone as she sat at home; desperately wanting Johnny to be by her side. She found herself lapsing into a deeper depression as the days went by. The grief was overwhelming as she remembered the pain.

After Debbie gathered her thoughts, she said, "Johnny would come home, and he was so worn out from working and playing golf, all he wanted to do was sit in silence. I would try to engage him in conversation, but he was tired from his day and couldn't offer the compassion I needed after being home all day sadly grieving. This caused a great strain on our marriage as we quietly retreated back down into the deep cavities of mourning."

Johnny thoughtfully says, "Debbie didn't like me being so quiet and didn't know what to do with me. When I did come out and speak, my words were filled with rage and anger. She so needed me to be there for her as she grieved quietly, cried, and talked about her special love for Uriah. Our two different methods of grieving caused us great strife in our marriage, and it deteriorated faster each day."

We had difficulty sleeping at night, sometimes sleeping only an hour at night. When we did sleep, it was from pure exhaustion. Other times, I would get up in the morning and sit on the edge of Uriah's bed and try to put my jeans on, and I would start crying because Uriah would never be able to put his jeans on again. The little things drove me crazy.

I kept thinking about all the 'nevers' that I would 'never' get to do with Uriah. In my victim impact statement to Joshua, the murderer, I listed all the things I would never get to do with my son again. Never play baseball again, never go to the beach again, and never work in the garden again. Never! Never! Never! The list was long. All the 'nevers' were constantly on my mind.

My relationship with Debbie continued to deteriorate. She became very lonely and started to worry about me relapsing into alcohol or drugs again. I had quit drinking and gotten off drugs just one year and ten days before Uriah died. My loyal commitment to God when Uriah was killed was to never drink or take drugs again. I felt strong that I would never break that commitment, and to this day, God has kept me strong, and I have not broken that promise. Unfortunately, I didn't communicate the commitment I had made to God to Debbie, and she was worried. She didn't feel she could cope with me on drugs again and started to feel like the whole situation was hopeless.

She began to have suicidal thoughts herself. Life had become unbearable, and the grief was overwhelming. One day she became so despondent, she drove to the edge of the lake and was going to drive the car into the water, but something kept her from doing so. Debbie was gently reminded of the near-death experience, years before Uriah was murdered, when she died on the living room couch during a massive grand mal seizure. I told her after the seizure that she had quit breathing for several minutes, and she was as "gray as the pavement." Her eyes were completely dilated, and her heart had stopped.

Debbie recalls, "I remember feeling completely alone and empty to the hollows of my bones. I had lost all hope of ever connecting to the world again. I remember my dog curled up by my feet on the couch and thinking she was the last living being who loved me unconditionally. During the seizure, my entire chest cavity arched way up, and my head and neck were thrust over the end of the couch. Johnny thought I'd had a massive heart attack.

"One minute I was on the couch, and then suddenly I was in heaven. I don't remember any dark tunnels or even how I got there. I just knew, when I arrived, that I was in heaven. I felt such sheer joy and love, almost overwhelming, as I stood in the middle of a beautiful meadow. I was a part of everything, and I felt such a profound sense of belonging. All my pain, shame, and loneliness were gone. I felt like I was let out of a torture chamber, and I was set free. I was just Debbie, as though God were saying, 'Debbie, you are loved and accepted no matter what you do, and I am always with you.' If you multiply the human love you have for someone a million times, it simply wouldn't even come close. It is hard to explain in earthly words, but it is definitely something I won't ever forget.

"During this near-death experience, it was as though the entire Twenty-Third Psalm had come to life before me. I was standing in the greenest, most beautiful, pasture with gently rolling hills. The grass was a vivid, beautiful green like nothing I have seen on earth. The large pool of water was so still, and I was so amazed that such a large amount of water could be so still. I felt complete freedom, joy, and tranquility like I had never experienced. I felt so accepted and released from all the pain. There was absolutely nothing I needed to do or change."

Then it hit me like a train: "I felt so relieved to know that God was so real and so powerful beyond anything I could have ever imagined. Up to this point in my life, my belief in God had been more wishful and hoping there was a God. There were times in my teens and twenties that I didn't believe in God at all. Now I was here in heaven, and I knew there was a God and that He had always been with me—always!

"When I arrived in heaven, a beautiful spiritual being named Tony was there to greet me. He had been a friend of my husband whom I had always disliked and treated with hostility, because I didn't have good feelings about him. The last time I had seen him, he was lying dead in an open coffin, and as I passed by the coffin I said to myself, *Tony, you got exactly what you deserved!* Then I felt bad because he had been murdered at the young age of thirty and left behind a wife and two children."

So there I was in heaven, looking into the vibrant, smiling face of Tony, and I saw what I believed to be the Christ that dwells within. This might sound odd, but all I can say is that once you have seen Christ, you know Him and will never forget Him. There simply are no words to describe Him. Tony and I communicated without speaking; we just knew each other's thoughts. I remember thinking, *This guy is the last person I would expect to meet in heaven*, and he would tilt his head back and laugh.

Anyway, Tony led me beside the still water and led me through the grassy pasture to some beautiful, multisided, columned buildings. The three buildings were full of light—light where you have no physical pain and where moving around requires no effort at all. What it showed me was how wrong I was about Tony, and it showed me his true spiritual beauty. As we moved through the second building, I had thoughts like, *So, this God stuff is really real, and heaven is really real, and people like me really do go to heaven*. Tony would laugh with joy at my amazement.

I felt so totally at ease and thought I belonged there forever. You would think I would have thought about my husband, parents, children, or at least my dog, but I didn't—I was just Debbie. I knew I was *home*. There was no room for sadness or pain.

Tony led me to the third and final building of light, only this time I saw three women gathered in front. They were so happy to see me and laughed as they chatted and greeted me. I am pretty sure one was my grandmother from pictures I had seen, but I wasn't sure who the other two women were. At that point, I felt like I wanted to stay, and I was enjoying the relaxing atmosphere of the three women, when suddenly, I was sucked back into my earthly body like a tremendously powerful vacuum was ripping across my body.

I felt my left shoulder ripping, and then the pain traveling down to my stomach. I have never felt such rage as the pain had a life all its own. I never knew such pain existed. I looked around the living room, and big men with raincoats (firemen) and paramedics were standing there. I started to rip off all the monitoring devices they had attached to my chest. I felt such rage; I could have probably hurt someone. I didn't want to be back here on earth. Every muscle in my body hurt, and I wanted so badly to be back in heaven. I wanted to feel the love, joy, and total acceptance where Christ resides within. It was a horrifying trip back to earth, and it took me almost a full year to let go of the anger and depression I experienced afterward.

So seven years later, I was sitting at this lake ready to drive my car into the lake, because we had lost Uriah, and I was reminded of that beautiful experience in heaven. I knew in my heart that God doesn't want us to take matters into our own hands. He wants us to trust Him, love Him, and give Him praise, and He will take care of the rest.

Debbie went on to say, "God gently intervened and reminded me that in doing harm to myself, I would be dishonoring Uriah and, for that matter, dishonoring God Himself. God wants us to trust Him with everything in our lives, and when we take matters into our own hands, He is saddened. He will give us a way out of our misery if we turn to Him and earnestly ask for help. With that, I drove out of the lake parking lot and went home. I knew that someday I would be with Christ in heaven on His terms and I would see Uriah again."

Johnny reflects, "When we both finally reached the stage of being so intensely sick with grief, feeling defeated, feeling hopeless, feeling suicidal, and tired of facing the battle that raged within us each day, we finally turned to therapy. It was recommended time after time by our pastor, our family, friends, and coworkers, but we kept ignoring it. I had strong feelings that a therapist was not going to know how I felt and be able to help me with my loss, so why waste the money? In actuality, it ended up saving my life and it saved our marriage."

We started off with couple's therapy, and we had several group sessions. This was helping us to see that other couples were facing the same problems we were experiencing and we could learn from them. This helped us to know we were not alone in our grief.

When you lose a child, it is common for parents to think no one else knows what they are going through. The grief is so raw, and the personal pain is focused on just them. When you get to the point where you can take a deep breath and listen to others, you find they are encountering the same feelings as you.

Debbie and I also spent individual hours in therapy discussing our own feelings and methods of grieving. We begin to have more compassion and empathy for each other. We realized we couldn't control or change each other, so we started being kinder to each other and finding small ways to spend time together in order to share our grief. We didn't try to change each other or "fix" each other. We practiced listening to each other without interruption and accepting with compassion the way we each chose to grieve. This gave us the relief and validation we both needed.

We could only control our own behaviors, and this technique seemed to make a big difference. Our marriage started to heal as we gently accepted each other's methods of grieving. We are not ashamed to say we attended therapy every week for years. This helped us move forward in baby steps to enjoy bits of life again. Our shattered hearts were finding bits and pieces of healing as we progressed; although we had not yet found the complete peace we needed, we were feeling better.

One important aspect of therapy Debbie and I discovered was that grief has five stages that each person may go through—not necessarily in order—but they were stages we could understand. "As we explored these five stages, we realized that these stages were common and normal behavior that almost every grieving person goes through with any loss. This gave us great comfort to know we were experiencing grief like everyone else. We were not alone. What a relief to know this was normal behavior. Maybe we weren't going crazy after all."

The five stages were developed by Elisabeth Kübler-Ross in her famous 1969 book, *On Death and Dying*.[10] She developed this model for terminally ill people, but it was soon adapted as stages everyone experiences as they grieve. Elisabeth Kübler-Ross made it clear in her writings that people can experience these stages of grief at different times, and they do not happen in any particular order. In fact, you may go through all of them over and over during the course of one day. With different bereavements, you may even skip some stages, depending on how serious the grief is affecting you. The five stages include:

Shock/Denial: The shock may leave you feeling numb, shattered, quiet, and unable to believe (denial) that someone you care about is gone. Even if we are told our loved one is gone, we can't really wrap our heads around the thought that they are not coming back. It is very common during this stage to imagine hearing their voice or even seeing them. This is a time when family and friends gather around you to help you through the shock of losing someone you love.

Debbie comments, "I saw Uriah in two visions/dreams the first year after he was gone. One dream was when I entered an eight-story building, and he was sitting there in a chair. He stood up, put his hands on me, and led me down the hall to a peach-colored room. A picture of Uriah was hanging on the wall; the very one that I had been crying over, and shockingly it came to life. I woke up and the Lord let me know he was okay.

"The other dream was Uriah showing me his heavenly house. I was in a log cabin looking out over a beautiful river. Oddly, the furniture was carved out of the logs attached to the wall. Uriah showed me around his eternal home, and he gave me comfort." Both dreams helped to give me the comfort I needed at the time.

Anger: This is a completely natural emotion and very common after someone dies. Death can appear to be so unfair, so cruel, especially if the death is of a child. When you feel someone died before their time or if you have future plans with them, it can be especially anger-provoking. It is also common to feel angry with ourselves for things we did or didn't do before they died, and it's even common for angry feelings to surface toward the loved one for dying.

Bargaining: This is the time when we are in such

pain that we find ourselves bargaining and making deals with ourselves: "If I had done this, my son wouldn't have died." "If I had not let her go to the movies, this wouldn't have happened." "If I had been closer to God, this wouldn't have happened." We "bargain" for different circumstances and additional "what ifs" to make us feel better, wishing we could go back and change the course of things in the hope it would have turned out differently.

Johnny says, "My grieving included self-blame of: *If Uriah had not been homeless at the age of nine, he might not have been in this situation*, to *If he had not been exposed to alcohol, he might have lived.* The "what ifs" can leave you feeling defeated.

Depression: This is a scary stage in which life can feel like it no longer has any meaning. Depression or sadness may come in waves over many months—or years, if left untreated. The sadness and longing for your loved one can cause great pain and loneliness. This pain can progress into suicidal ideation, so it is important to get professional help if the sadness or depression continues for a time. This is a scary time for family members if you withdraw into yourself. They worry and wonder if you will get so despondent that you may hurt yourself. Be sure to communicate that you simply need some quiet time to process your loss and spend time with God. This will help family members understand and not worry so much.

Acceptance: The grieving process comes in waves, and it can feel like life will never be right again. Your life has changed, and a new lifestyle has to be developed. Gradually, people find that the pain eases with time and it is possible to accept what has happened. We may never "get over" the death of someone we care about, but we can accept that it has happened and learn to go on again, while keeping the memories of those who died close to us in our hearts.

A grieving person may start with shock or denial and not necessarily go in the order of the five stages by becoming angry next. In fact, most people move back and forth between the stages, and some people get "stuck" in one stage, like anger or depression, and unfortunately never get to acceptance. There is help for anyone feeling like they are stuck somewhere in the grieving process.

Johnny mentions, "In our journey of grief, we learned that by praying to God, it actually helped us through each stage and gave us greater peace. We learned to trust in Him, hoping He would eventually deliver us from the intense pain and give us a certain level of peace. No, we will never forget our son, Uriah, and we will always continue to miss him, yet we started to feel a bit of serenity where we could begin to cope and enjoy bits of life again. The most difficult part was giving ourselves permission to laugh again, because we felt so guilty that Uriah wasn't there to laugh with us."

As we progressed through group therapy and individual therapy, we felt our shattered hearts slowly start to mend. Gradually, our marriage was starting to heal, and we were settling into some semblance of peace within our relationship.

And then the murder trial for the man who killed our son was scheduled, and everything changed.

Put on the whole armor of God, that you may be able to stand against the wiles of the devil.

Ephesians 6:11 NKJV

Give all your worries and cares to God,

for he cares about you.

1 Peter 5:7

Chapter 7

Hangtown Creek Murder Trial

The trial was scheduled for April 1998, seven months after Uriah was murdered. We both felt anxiety, not knowing for sure what would happen. The attorneys and district attorney eased our minds by giving us options. We could settle for a twenty-year sentence for the murderer and avoid a trial, or we could go through a trial, hoping for a longer sentence. They mentioned that a jury trial could go on for weeks or months, and the case could end up in a mistrial.

We felt that Joshua Smith, the murderer, deserved more time than twenty years in prison, but we also knew a jury trial could grant him less time or the jury could conclude in a hung jury or a mistrial, and Joshua would be set free. The thought of him being out on the streets was not an option for us.

We decided as a family not to go through the pain and suffering of a trial. The thought of seeing pictures of Uriah murdered, his throat slit, and lying face-down in the creek was too much for us to endure. We had already been through enough pain and hurt, and so, to avoid any further suffering, our family decided to accept the twenty-year sentence, knowing the murderer would go to prison right away. There was a certain amount of peace knowing that he was incarcerated and we didn't have to relive all the horror.

The courts scheduled the sentencing date for May, two weeks after the trial court appearance. We would then have a chance to publicly make our impact statements, speaking them directly to Joshua. Our whole family showed up wearing pictures of Uriah on their lapels and spoke about the pain they each felt and how his death had impacted their lives.

Johnny mentioned that his impact statement was divided up into three different parts: 1) The impact on his life, 2) his feelings regarding the sentence, 3) his only son, his only child, and the things he would miss.

The Impact on My Life

Looking directly at the murderer, I said to him, "The impact on my life has changed me forever. As his dad, life will never be the same for me. I am not able to sleep for more than one hour at a time without waking up. I have…

No appetite

No energy

A bad attitude

A poor attitude of support for my wife

No cares about anything

No focus on anything

Less productivity at work

Panic attacks, resulting in days off from work

A hard time holding a conversation

Financial trouble

Had to go to therapy for help

Extreme sensitivity about everything

An inability to stop crying or feeling depressed

No will to live when I wake up in the morning

My Feelings Regarding the Sentence

Johnny looked directly into the killer's eyes and said, "Nine months ago, you didn't give my son, Uriah, any choice when you took his life from him. If I wasn't a man of God, I would prefer to sentence you myself to see how tough you really are. You weren't defending yourself against Uriah—you meant to kill him. I know it and you know it!

"Uriah never did anything to hurt you. He even tried to help you by finding you a place to stay overnight. Uriah even stayed out with you one night so you wouldn't be all alone. I don't feel sorry for you one bit. I wouldn't even waste my time to walk across this room to spit on you. You just aren't worth it. The only news I want to hear about you is that you got that third strike against you, and you have to spend the rest of your sick life in jail." I had so much anger and rage inside me. God help me!

My Only Son, My Only Child, and the Things I Will Miss

Johnny took a deep breath, looked directly at the killer, and said, "I wish you were older and had kids of your own. Then you might be able to understand what you have taken from us." Johnny started to shake with anger and rage as his voice cracked.

"Uriah and I were very close. We did everything together. Here are some of the things I will miss.

Never getting to work in the yard with Uriah again.

Never bathing the dogs together again.

Never walking down the street together again.

Never going to Berkley and getting pizza by the slice again.

Never driving to work together again.

Never getting to tickle each other again.

Never roughhousing together again.

Never getting to pull pranks on each other again.

Never getting to cook dinner together again.

Never going to a movie together again.

Never getting to go swimming together again or going to the beach (Uriah's favorite place).

Never getting to footrace with each other again.

Never getting to play golf or the guitar together again.

Never getting to see him finish his music career.

Never getting to talk to him about girls again.

Never getting to see him buy his first car.

Never getting to see Uriah find love and get married.

"When you killed my son, you took part of my heart with him. Part of me died that day. I lived for Uriah. I was his dad, and I was there for him no matter what.

"I loved Uriah more than I love life." Holding up an enlarged picture of Uriah, I said, "I will miss his beautiful smile and how he would look me eye to eye and say, 'I love you, Daddy-O'!" Around the courtroom, you could hear muffled cries and sobs.

Joshua, the murderer, kept his head down the whole time I was talking. He acted tough, like he didn't care, and he just didn't look at us.

Debbie got up to give her impact statement, and in her soft, sincere voice, she said, "It is very important that you know that Uriah was very dear to me. As his stepmother, I cherished my time with him. We had many very special moments, and this loss has created a huge void in my life. It will never be the same." Joshua looked at her briefly and then put his head back down.

When everyone had given their impact statements, the guards led Joshua out of the courtroom to begin his twenty-year sentence.

The next morning, the local newspaper published separate articles on both the murderer and Uriah McDaniel.

"Hangtown Creek Murderer Gets 20 Years: One Young Man Kills Another Young Man"

The local newspaper article reported that Joshua Smith was sentenced to twenty years in prison for killing Uriah McDaniel.

The article read: "An 18-year-old man who bludgeoned and stabbed a 20-year-old man, for reasons that remain known only to him and possibly the victim, pleaded no contest Wednesday and agreed to a 20-year state prison sentence."

"Joshua Smith, now 19, killed Uriah Ulysses McDaniel along Hangtown Creek in the early morning hours of September 10, 1997. Smith previously contended it was self-defense. As trial opening arguments were to begin Wednesday in County Superior Court, the defense, the district attorney's office and the victim's family instead settled on a 20-year sentence for manslaughter and other crimes Joshua committed in the last year. Smith, clean shaven and in his blue blazer and tie for the morning sentencing, reappeared in the afternoon in orange prison fatigues and shackles to hear statements from the victim's family."

In an emotional session, McDaniel's two aunts, grandmother, mother, stepmother, and father spoke. All wore pictures of McDaniel on their lapels.

"This morning as I sat in court and heard about your rights and your choices," Aunt Pam said. "I wondered how many rights and choices you gave to Uriah, as he screamed for you to stop, don't do it."

Smith sat listening, sometimes looking at the speakers, sometimes looking away.

The only witness to what had happened was a fourteen-year-old runaway who testified at Smith's preliminary hearing. The girl said she had only known

Uriah McDaniel for about one month and she'd met Smith for the first time the day before the killing.

Around 9 p.m. that night, the three attended a party during which McDaniel, Smith, and the fourteen-year-old girl were all drinking. When the party broke up around midnight, the three young people wandered around Placerville, looking for a place to spend the night. The girl said she sensed Smith was jealous that McDaniel had kissed and hugged her as they walked through town.

When they came to the bridge that crosses the creek near Main Street, Smith led McDaniel away into the thick brush.

Soon after the young men disappeared into the darkness, the girl said she heard a *thump* and McDaniel scream, "Josh, stop!"

"I heard splashing around. I heard Uriah screaming," she said.

Minutes later, a blood-splattered Smith came back to the bridge where the girl was waiting. "I knew something was wrong when Uriah didn't come back," she said. Placerville police discovered McDaniel's body the next morning at 10:45 a.m. lying in the middle of the shallow creek behind Main Street. His head was badly beaten, and he had multiple stab wounds, including a deep wound to his neck.

Officers canvassed the downtown area questioning people, even at one point speaking to Smith on Main Street, but did not have any information to link him to the killing at that time. By 3 p.m. Smith was arrested at an apartment complex. Smith pleaded not guilty to murder charges and was held without bail.

The deputy district attorney said, from all witnesses interviewed and evidence gathered on McDaniel, "There is nothing to show anything but a passive guy. He never expressed any violent tendencies."

Smith, however, "is a violent person," who allegedly stabbed another acquaintance a month before killing McDaniel. During the McDaniel murder investigation, the earlier stabbing victim came forward and said, "Several friends ran out of gas in route to Los Angeles. One friend got into a fight with Smith's girlfriend, and Smith, allegedly high on methamphetamine, stabbed him."

Now Smith, settling the McDaniel case without a trial, will not have to explain why he killed Uriah.

The superior court judge said, "Only you alone know what happened."

Under violent-crime sentencing guidelines, Smith must serve at least 85 percent of his twenty-year sentence, or seventeen years. It is not what he deserves—everyone on the prosecution side believes he deserves more—but a jury might have convicted him for less. In addition to killing McDaniel, Smith pleaded no contest to an armed robbery and assaulting two acquaintances. He was also convicted of threatening a jail deputy and saying he would blow up his house.

Finally, the judge addressed Smith. "I hope, Mr. Smith, that during your time in prison you will appreciate the void left in the McDaniel family. Their lives and what you have put them through is something you will have to live with, and I hope you will have time to think about how you can change your ways, while you are in prison."

As sobs filled the air, the bailiffs walked the shackled Smith past the courtroom full of McDaniel's family and friends.

"Family Remembers Murdered Son"

In the local newspaper article, Johnny McDaniel spoke about his son, Uriah Ulysses McDaniel, who, at the young age of twenty years old, was stabbed and bludgeoned to death in Hangtown Creek.

The motive remains unexplained, but it is clear McDaniel was deprived of the chance to outlive his youthful transgressions and shine as a promising musician.

Several family members said Uriah was going through a rebellious stage, common for his age, which involved too much drinking and partying. This, in a town as small as Placerville, unfortunately, put him in a circle that included his murderer.

However, the prosecutor of this case, said from all witnesses interviewed and the evidence considered on McDaniel, "There is nothing to show anything but a passive guy. He never expressed any violent tendencies."

The family said Uriah had a drinking problem, but he also had a real heart for homeless people—and in this case, it possibly might have cost him his life.

Johnny McDaniel, Uriah's dad, said his son had studied karate for several years as a child and was adept at defending himself. Johnny believed alcohol impaired his ability to defend himself that night, allowing Smith to attack and kill him.

The family said it was typical of Uriah's nature when once he brought Smith to his aunt's home when he needed a place to stay. Uriah's aunt said, "I looked at this guy and he was gross," and I said, "You can stay Uriah, but he has to go." Uriah refused to stay—he wouldn't leave his friend alone. That's the kind of person Uriah was. We thought that since Uriah was left alone and homeless at the young age of nine, he had developed a soft heart for those without a home.

Grandmother Joan said, "Uriah used to sneak homeless people into her house to sleep on the couch. I would get up in the morning and come out to the living room and find a stranger on the couch. He had such a kind heart."

The family said Uriah was a natural musician who wrote songs and music that he played on his guitar and piano. His dad, John McDaniel, said the South Carolina band Pegasus wanted to buy one of his songs, but Uriah didn't want to sell it; he wanted to keep it for himself. "He'd write a song and play it for hours in the bedroom on his guitar," said stepmother Deborah McDaniel, "Then he would come out and play it on the piano. I asked him, 'Where did you learn to play the piano?' He said, 'I don't play the piano.' He was playing by ear and had such a natural ability. He amazed us."

Recordings of his music were played at the funeral. More than three hundred people attended the September 16, 1997, memorial.

Deborah McDaniel said Uriah's favorite movies were *Braveheart*, *The Shawshank Redemption*, and *Dead Poet's Society*. "In *Dead Poet's Society*, there's a part about seizing the day, following your dream. The day after he saw the movie, he went out and traded his grandfather's 1956 Gibson guitar, a family heirloom, for an electric guitar and a mandolin. Deborah and John McDaniel laughed at the memory."

Johnny McDaniel, who lives in Oakland, said his son displayed a kindness and gentleness beyond his young age. "We used to walk around Berkeley. I didn't like him being there at night, so sometimes I walked with him. He loved Big Slice Pizza, and he would buy two slices, walk down the street, then take a napkin and hand it to a homeless person. Or he would leave it on top of a napkin on a trash can so some hungry person didn't have to dig through the trash for something to eat." That was Uriah.

They recalled another instance when Uriah picked up stray dogs, including a Great Dane named Bubba, which they still have. Uriah found Bubba on the street, all skin and bones and dehydrated. Deborah, Uriah's stepmother, said, "I never could have imagined that Bubba would outlive Uriah." Johnny says, "Now that dog is super-special to me."

"It's been nine months since Uriah was murdered, and we cry all the time and pray every morning," said Deborah McDaniel, struggling to find the right words. "When it happens to you, the violence . . . seeing what happened to him . . . getting the funeral together . . . I still wander through the grocery store looking for things he liked to eat: smoked oysters, cream soda . . ."

The day Smith was sentenced, Uriah McDaniel's birth mother, Susie. said, "My son's friends called me and came over to my house in cut-off shorts and T-shirts." Susie said, "You can't wear those clothes to court. Come into Uriah's room and get some of his clothes and wear them." It was so heartwarming to see his friends in court wearing Uriah's clothes. It was almost comforting.

The sentencing was all over, the newspaper articles died off, Joshua was sentenced to prison, and now it was time for us to return home.

I have told you all this so that you may have peace in me.

Here on earth you will have many trials and sorrows.

But take heart, because I have overcome the world.

John 16:33

Chapter 8

Forgiveness Seems Impossible

Following the sentencing of the murderer, we arrived home feeling some peace that Joshua was in prison for twenty years; yet we still didn't have our son, Uriah. We still had to grieve our loss and go on living. Life just didn't seem fair. We painfully began the routine of home life and work as we continued our therapy. We learned that having a routine was very important to our healing.

Johnny explains, "Just seeing the murderer in court brought up some of the old rage and hatred inside me. Giving the victim-impact statements proved to be a cleansing time, letting Joshua know how his brutal actions had affected our lives, and for that matter, the rest of our lives. It was an emotional time for all of us."

My question was, "What is a person to do with all this frustration inside?" The therapists mentioned finding ways to relax and release the pent-up frustration. They suggested listening to relaxing music, breath training to rid the body of anxiety, or any form of exercise such as golfing, yoga, walking, or running. Some people have even participated in 'rage room' sessions, where you take a baseball bat and smash things to vent your pent-up anger. I chose golf as a way to help relax my mind.

These suggestions may work for a momentary

short release, but the only option to true forgiveness is found through Jesus. We needed to be set free from all the anger and hatred that was consuming us. Saying you are going to 'forgive' is the start of a whole lifestyle change, and Jesus can help.

Debbie and I started sharing our story with others as much as possible. A friend from work gave me a brochure on a three-day workshop, coming up the following weekend, called "Free the Heart." I was having one of those depressing kind of days when I was tired of dealing with my painful grief. Even with therapy, I still had days when the devil had me by the throat, ready to torture me. Feeling defeated, I thought, *Maybe we should give this a try. It couldn't hurt us any more than we are hurting now.* We were so tired of suffering.

This three-day workshop called "Free the Heart" had a subtitle: "Trust, Safety, Truth, Freedom, Forgiveness, and Love." As we sat down for the Friday night session, the speaker said, "You will only get out of this workshop what you are willing to put into it." The instructor also said, "Trust the process as you go through the workshop. Be patient with yourself."

The Friday night of the workshop was a time of everyone sharing why they were there attending the workshop. There were people who had been molested, been in bad accidents, been harmed by others, been divorced or lost a spouse, and a few who had lost a child to an accident, but we were the only ones who had lost a child to murder. It was surreal to learn why so many people were in such pain and why it was so difficult to go on living. We all had different stories, but we all had insufferable pain. Once again, we discovered we were no longer alone with our pain.

On Saturday we spent time in group sessions and completed exercises on anger management. We all blew up balloons and wrote a word on it, like *rage*, *anger*, *hate*, or *violence*, then we threw all the balloons out in the middle of the floor. Johnny mentions, "I blew up about sixty balloons and wrote all these words on the—things that had plagued me for months. When we got done, the whole room was two to three feet deep in balloons, and it looked like an ugly cesspool of suffering. As we madly popped all the balloons and screamed, it released some of the pent-up anger we all had within us. It felt good to release some of our stress and do it with other people who felt the same."

On Sunday of the workshop, we reached the 'forgiveness and love' portion of the program. "I wasn't very crazy about attending this session," says Johnny. "I felt uncomfortable as we started the exercise. I actually wanted to run out of the room, but an invisible hand gently pressed down on my shoulder keeping me there. Later, I realized this invisible hand must have been God, because no one else was near me at the time."

We were asked to choose a partner and pretend they were the person we needed to forgive. In my case, I was choosing a partner and pretending they were Joshua, the murderer of my son. As I looked into my partner's eyes, I had nothing but hatred for him. He felt my angry energy and backed away a step or two, not certain what I was about to do. He knew I was carrying a lot of rage and anger, and he didn't want to be on the receiving end if I decided to hit or throw a punch at him.

The instructor asked me to look at my partner and say, "I forgive you for murdering my son." There wasn't one bone in my body that wanted to say those words. Yet a small, quiet voice in my head said, *You came here to get help, so give it a try.*

This was difficult, and the words seemed to get stuck in my throat. I finally said them, but I didn't mean them at all. This was obvious to the instructor, and she had me say it again, and again, and again, until the words were coming out with some true meaning of forgiveness. My voice started to soften, and my voice quavered as I broke down and cried. My class partner put his arms around me until my raging sobs subsided. When I lifted my head, my eyes saturated with tears, I felt an inner peace flow into my body.

My hatred was lifting, my anger was more controlled, and a Spirit inside me was giving me the greatest peace I had ever felt. I was told this was the "Holy Spirit," giving me the peace and courage I needed to go on. God was with me, Jesus was with me, and the Holy Spirit was within me. As I repeated the words of forgiveness over and over, I felt God working through me, giving me complete calmness and healing.

We read in Scripture these words by Jesus: "Come to Me, all you who labor and are heavy laden, and I will give you rest. Take My yoke upon you and learn from Me, for I am gentle and lowly in heart, and you will find rest for your souls" (Matthew 11:28–29 NKJV).

Psychologists generally define *forgiveness* as a conscious, deliberate decision to release feelings of resentment or vengeance toward a person or group who has harmed you, regardless of whether or not they actually deserve your forgiveness.

Toxic forgiveness is when you attempt to forgive someone when you still have painful hurt or haven't gotten 100 percent closure concerning the situation. This can cause trauma or erode your mental health.[11] A person needs to understand that unconditional forgiveness from the heart comes only from the Lord. He gives us the strength and peace to forgive.

Looking back after all these years, Johnny says, "This was the turning point for me to want to live again. I was starting to believe 100 percent in God and find forgiveness in my heart for the man who took my son's life. I was starting to find some inner peace where I felt calm again."

Debbie quietly mentions, "This type of workshop was very helpful in putting us back on our feet again. Just being able to talk with others who had been through a tragedy connected us together in a way only God can do. We finally started to grab hold of the hope that we would survive this difficult time. It was a lifesaver."

When you lose a child, you are part of a club you never want to join, but Romans 8:28 states, "And we know that all things work together for good to those who love God, to those who are the called according to His purpose" (NKJV). God allows us to comfort others with the same comfort we have received from Him.[12] As time passes, we will see flashes of God's purpose.

Uriah, my son, saved a fourteen-year-old girl from possible rape or worse, and he gave his life while doing so. Johnny also says, "Uriah also brought about my salvation. One month after he died, Debbie and I dedicated our lives to the Lord. I might never have drawn close to God without him sacrificing his life. I had a childhood with no father present, a brother who beat me up every day of my life, a failed marriage, a period of alcoholism and drug use. God protected me through my childhood and early adult life. But He also gifted me with a son, who happened to be murdered and taken from me, and in this process, I drew closer to the Lord Jesus. Since that day, I have stayed committed to the Lord to follow Him, love Him, and praise Him every day of the rest of my life."

Johnny concludes that, "I feel this workshop actually saved my life, along with the hours and hours of weekly counseling. I felt God starting to work through me, and after completing this three-day workshop, I felt like I had a good start on a new lease on life. I proceeded to attend the same workshop a few more times. It was a great help to me."

Forgiveness doesn't mean that what happened to you was okay. Forgiveness doesn't mean you become friends with or agree with the murderer. Forgiveness isn't an event; it is a change in lifestyle. By forgiving, you never forget the child you gave life to or all the memories you cherish. Forgiveness means you make an intentional decision to let go of resentment and anger. Forgiveness frees you from the bitterness and resentment that rules your life.

Even when you say you are forgiving someone, you may still have negative thoughts that spring up when you least expect them. Saying you are going to "forgive" is the start of a whole lifestyle change, and only Jesus can help.

Then Peter came to him and asked,

"Lord, how often should I forgive someone who sins against me? Seven times? No, not seven times," Jesus replied, "but seventy times seven."

Matthew 18:21–22

Chapter 9

Go in There and Teach

After attending several Free the Heart three-day workshops, we were eventually invited to actually join the staff, without pay, as they proceeded to develop a prison ministry. This was the beginning of six years of continued healing. We joined the Free the Heart organization to become part of a prison outreach, where we go into prisons to present the three-day workshop on forgiveness. We went to male and female prisons all over the United States, but mainly on the West Coast. It was one of the many things we did to honor Uriah's memory.

As the main income provider for Debbie and me, this was a difficult decision for us to make. My job as a construction estimator had been paying me over six figures annually, so I was torn between giving up our financial stability and following what I felt God wanted me to do. As I prayed, God shook me up by saying, *Go in there and TEACH it to them.* This simple, but bold message told me I needed to go in there and teach the prisoners about trust, love, and forgiveness through Jesus Christ. This bold message shook me to the core, and with that I decided to give up my high-paying job and trust that the Lord would supply us with income. I was going to follow Jesus.

Debbie said, "After the first year of prison ministry,

I decided to work in a long-term care facility in Oakland, which helped pay our basic bills. I ran the front office and took care of the residents' needs by getting them lunch tickets, a newspaper, or other essentials. When I could get away, I spent two years following the Pastor Benny Hinn crusades to different locations in the United States to sing and worship in the eight-hundred-to-one-thousand-person chorus. The healing power of God I felt during the Crusades helped me heal my own wounds. This was something I enjoyed, and to this day, I have fond memories of singing in that chorus."

Many people know Pastor Benny Hinn from his fifty years of preaching, healing, teaching, and writing bestselling books. At the young age of twenty-four, Benny received a vision of people falling into a roaring inferno and heard the words: "If you do not preach, every soul that falls will be your responsibility." Four days later, his lifetime stuttering problem disappeared, and Benny has been preaching for fifty years since that message.[13]

Johnny commented, "When I wasn't traveling to prison workshops, I worked for a property management company doing maintenance work, cleaning, and landscaping. One day the manager asked me to pull some weeds. I took a look at those weeds and thought, *I don't want to pull weeds for a lousy fifteen dollars an hour*. I heard God's voice in my ear say firmly, *All service is for ME*. I humbled myself and pulled the weeds . . . happy to serve our Lord. In the future, I never questioned anything He asked me to do for Him. The Lord does not want us to be arrogant, but rather to be of service to Him.

While following what the Lord wanted us to do, we were being provided for adequately. We never went without food, and we always had enough money to pay our bills. We were among thirty other staff members of the Free the Heart workshops, and we began the prison ministry by visiting various male and female prisons, offering three-day workshops on trust, love, and forgiveness. We usually visited each prison three times a year that allowed us to come in and give the workshop.

The first time the staff went into a prison, Debbie and I were a little nervous. Among the crowd of burly men, with tattooed bodies and scars, were sexual molesters, robbers, and murderers, some of whom were serving life sentences. Any one of them could take us out with one crushing blow, and the look on some of their faces confirmed our thoughts. We were nothing to them, until we started talking about our own son, Uriah, who had been murdered. Then the energy in the room changed. The prisoners got quiet and listened intently to every word. They stared at us and became very curious about why we were there talking to them. They couldn't believe anyone would come in and talk about forgiveness or even give them the time of day after what they had done. Forgiving someone for the crime of murder seemed impossible.

As we went through the program, we followed the same protocol of the previous workshops by having a Friday night connection meeting, discussing why each of them were there for the workshop and what they hoped to get out of it. We talked about how forgiveness and God's love were available to each of them. All they had to do was ask. Most of the prisoners were somewhat confused by this, but they were intent on listening. They were puzzled why we would come in, after our own son was murdered, and talk to them about forgiveness.

We discussed how each person could ask God to forgive them and repent of all their sins. Many people believe that bigger sins are harder to forgive. God will forgive any sin, big or small, but what He does ask of us is to go forth and sin no more. Yes, if you break the law, you will have to serve your time. Yet, if you turn to God, you will do so with a certain level of peace and understanding. Some of the prisoner's faces began to soften. We saw a glimmer of hope in some of their eyes. They listened intently.

During the last day of the workshop, Johnny said, "I was giving the talk on forgiving the murderer, and I mentioned to this class of fifteen burly, tattooed, muscle-bound men that the 'hardest part about forgiveness is forgiving oneself for hurting someone else'."

This one three-hundred-pound man, in a cut-off T-shirt that showed off all his tattoos running up and down his arms, jumped up from his chair and came directly toward me. At first glance, I wasn't sure what the prisoner was up to. The guards jumped to attention and stepped toward me for protection. As the big, burly man approached the front of the room, I felt myself holding my breath, like this might be my last one, but then I could see the tears in his eyes, and I waved off the guards. As he approached, God whispered to just reach out to him, and when I did, he fell to his knees, buried his face in my chest, and just sobbed. We couldn't help but cry with him. Here was this big, burly man, in prison for life, burying his face in my chest, finally releasing all his tension and stress. You could tell he felt genuine remorse over what he had done. It was one moment I will never forget, and to this day, it still brings tears to my eyes. That is the true power of God and forgiveness.

At the next prison, we experienced another life-changing moment. A man named Grizzly, serving a life sentence for murder, was very intimidating, standing tall at six-foot-nine and weighing about 350 pounds. He was a giant black man whom everyone respected out of fear of what he might do to them. I had just finished my talk on forgiveness and how Debbie and I had forgiven the murderer of our son. He walked up to the stage and said, "You give me hope that my victim will someday forgive me."

I said, "If you raped, beat up, murdered, or molested your victim, in reality, your victim will probably never come in to forgive you." Very few victims in the world actually physically visit a perpetrator and offer them forgiveness. It just doesn't happen very often. You have to forgive yourself through Jesus Christ. Most prisoners actually believe they cannot be forgiven for what they have done to their victims, but there is nothing God won't forgive you for in your life. You have to repent, believe that Jesus died for your sins on the cross, and ask for forgiveness of your sins.

He will forgive you. You then go forth, believing in God and sin no more. It doesn't work if you ask for forgiveness and then continue to sin over and over. You have to be "born again," giving up your old life and turning to a new life in Jesus. He loves you more than any human possibly can. He is the only One who can forgive you completely. It is the love He has for each of His children. The Scripture says, "For all have sinned and fall short of the glory of God" (Romans 3:23 NKJV).

Johnny recounts another prison experience: "In one of our male prisons, I encountered a man named Conrad. You didn't mess with Conrad. No one in prison messed with Conrad. He weighed 240 pounds and had eyes that sent chills down my spine. He was one who had murdered another man, and he actually scared me. I was doing an exercise of role-playing where you touch the prisoner's hand and start saying, 'I forgive you for murdering my son, and I want you to forgive yourself.' On this particular day, I decided to call Conrad up and role-play that I was his victim's dad, and as I grabbed his hands, I felt myself start to shake. When I said the words, 'Conrad, I forgive you for murdering my son, and I want you to forgive yourself,' I looked into his eyes and saw he was crying. He had never heard those words before.

In the next instant, Conrad grabbed my hands and said, "I want you to be Larry, the man I murdered." Then he said the same words to me: "Larry, please forgive me for killing you." He then grabbed me and broke down and sobbed while he shook to the core. When he quit sobbing, he said, "I have been in here ten years, and this is the first time I have cried. I now have hope for the first time in my life." It was quiet in the room as this mountain of a man cried. This gave other prisoners permission to feel and cry, too. Those prisoners who gave their lives to Jesus will spend eternity in heaven. God does forgive those who earnestly ask for it.

The love and forgiveness work that happened during the prison ministry was beyond words. Anyone can ask for forgiveness or give forgiveness and heal the broken human spirit. God is a loving and just God.

The workshops became something the prisoners looked forward to as they asked when we would return. One man shared that he was ready to commit suicide and didn't want to live anymore until he heard we were coming to the prison. He decided not to hurt himself because we were scheduled to visit. The prison ministry changed lives, saved lives, and broke down barriers. Our ministry saved hundreds of lives during those six years.

After six years of prison ministry, I was having dinner with some of the staff members. Linda, a great friend and fellow worker, looked across the table and said, "Johnny, you have been teaching for six years. Isn't it about time you went to physically forgive the murderer of your son?" It hit me like a ton of bricks. I had forgiven Joshua, the murderer, in my mind and on paper, but it had never occurred to me to do it in person.

It became apparent that after all these years, it was time for us to quit talking about forgiveness and "walk the talk." We had forgiven Joshua, the murderer, on paper and in our minds, over and over, but we had never considered visiting him in prison. We had done this prison ministry work to honor Uriah's name and follow what God wanted us to do.

Yet our faith in God was directing us to physically visit him in person and forgive him face-to-face. My mind kept swirling with the words in Mark 11:25–

26: "And whenever you stand praying, if you have anything against anyone, forgive him, that your Father in heaven may also forgive you your trespasses. But if you do not forgive, neither will your Father in heaven forgive your trespasses" (NKJV).

"These words really hit home with me," said Johnny. "I definitely wanted God to forgive me for all the sins I had committed against Him, so we decided to move ahead."

For most of us, forgiveness is extremely hard work. No one likes being hurt by another person. The loss of a loved one to a killer, who took that precious life from us, can only be held in the hands of God for healing and forgiveness.[14] Most of us harbor those hurt feelings inside us, unable to release them. We may lose sleep, struggling to find peace and let it go. We think we have the right to harbor ill feelings against someone who hurt us. Only God can help us let go, only God can give us the strength to trust, and only God can lead us toward true forgiveness.

There is no question that forgiveness work is hard—very hard. It can take years if Jesus isn't helping us. Yet it is much harder to live under the toxic poison of not forgiving another person. Unforgiveness is like drinking poison and expecting the murderer to die. The real problem with this is that you are the only one who suffers as you hold on to the hurt. Chronic anger enduring for a long period of time leads to depression, unhappiness, and sometimes more hate and more crimes. Chronic anger can lead to family issues, job loss, alcoholism, drug use, or car accidents. Chronic anger can also lead to medical issues, such as high blood pressure, anxiety disorders, serious digestive problems, skin disorders, and even heart problems. Living under the umbrella of unforgiveness can poison your life.

It was time for us to face the maximum-security prisoner in Pelican Bay State Prison and offer "forgiveness." Could we actually do it after all these years? Debbie and I decided to write Joshua Smith a letter.

Do not let the sun go down on your wrath,

nor give place to the devil.

Ephesians 4:26–27 NKJV

Make allowance for each other's faults,

and forgive anyone who offends you.

Remember, the Lord forgave you,

so you must forgive others.

Colossians 3:13

Chapter 10

Releasing the Prisoner Within

The time had come to walk the talk and forgive Joshua, the one who took our son from us, and forgive him in person.

Debbie says, "I felt the need to forgive Joshua long before Johnny did. I knew in my heart what needed to be done. When Johnny and I attended the Parents of Murdered Children meetings, we heard horrible stories of abuse, torture, and murder. I learned to be grateful that we knew who had killed Uriah and that our son's body had been found the next day. I was grateful the murderer was in custody and sentenced to twenty years in prison. As I listened to other parents talk about never finding their child's body, or never finding out who murdered their child, knowing they could still be out there walking around, I felt blessed that we had answers to most of our questions."

For Johnny, "I kept remembering that Scripture that says something like, remember, God will not forgive you of your sins, if you don't first forgive anyone you are holding a grudge or resentment toward. God shows His love and fairness when it comes to forgiveness, but you have to do your work, too."

For Johnny, as he looks back, "Forgiveness was really hard work. I needed to forgive over and over, only to have it rear its ugly head again. At times, I felt I had finally forgiven Joshua, only to have evil thoughts spring up in my mind. This is the devil trying to take a stronghold on God's work of forgiveness. We always have to remember that God is stronger than anything the devil can dish out. That is why God says you need to forgive seventy times seven. He knows us and knows negative thoughts can reappear at a moment's notice."

Most of us may feel we want a sincere apology from the person who murdered our child. We are certainly entitled to one, but usually that apology never comes. Even if they do apologize, it might not be sincere enough. We have just lost a son or daughter, and the words of an apology may seem empty in our hearts. The murderer might not even feel remorse in their heart and might not be fully aware of the damage they have caused us and our family.

The change in lifestyle is turning to God every minute, every hour, and every day for the rest of your life. He will change your life and bring out the good. As is stated in Romans 8:28, "And we know that God causes everything to work together for the good of those who love God and are called according to his purpose for them."

With everything in life, there is a season. God revealed to us that "your prison ministry was for a season, but your testimony is for forever." After eight years of healing, which included nine hundred hours of therapy, attending the Free the Heart workshops, and six years teaching the workshop in prisons, now it was time to write that letter of forgiveness to Joshua, the very man who had killed our son.

Joshua was serving his twenty-year sentence in Pelican Bay State Prison, a super-max prison facility in Crescent City, California. The prison opened in 1989 and holds 2,380 prisoners, with 1,056 solitary confinement cells organized into 132 eight-cell pods. Each cell contains a concrete ledge with a foam pad for a bed, a steel combination sink and toilet, and two concrete cubes that serve as a desk and chair. Armed guards monitor the cells from central control booths.[15] Pelican Bay was noted for housing the hard criminals.

As of March 2022, 60 percent of the 1,852 people incarcerated at Pelican Bay State Prison were Level IV, or maximum-security, prisoners, with the remaining population being Level I (minimum-security) and Level II prisoners. This prison has the reputation of holding some of the most notorious criminals, such as Charles Manson and dangerous CRIPS and Mafia members.[16] This was not a friendly place to go and hang out.

After praying and some deliberate thoughts, Debbie wrote down these faithful words:

January 2004

Dear Joshua:

Johnny and I are writing to you to let you know that though the last seven years since Uriah's death have been enormously painful, we want you to know that we forgive you completely. We harbor no ill-feelings toward you.

You are in our daily prayers, and I hope you find meaning and purpose in your life after all you have been through. Don't give up on God; He loves you and is not done with you.

As Johnny and I have shared our story with others, many people have been helped. We do prison outreach through an organization called Free the Heart and go to prisons to spend three days doing a workshop with the prisoners. It's one of the many things we do to honor Uriah's memory. He was an extremely sensitive person, and I know in my heart of hearts that he would want you to be happy. Uriah and I had talks about how important God is and what it would be like in heaven with Jesus.

For the first two years after Uriah died, my husband and I were both suicidal. Johnny now says he was not suicidal because his son was murdered, but because he couldn't forgive.

We would like to come see you and forgive you in person if you would allow that. Please contact your warden for arrangements.

Please accept our forgiveness and forgive yourself. We've all done something, usually many things, wrong and are in need of God's forgiveness. I hope that you find some measure of peace and that no matter what you have done, your life has meaning no matter where you are. I hope that things get a little easier for you.

God bless you, Joshua. Again, you and your family are in our prayers.

Sincerely,

Johnny & Debbie McDaniel

We sent the letter and waited, thinking we might not ever hear back from him. Yet to our surprise, six months later, Joshua responded with the following letter:

June 1, 2004

Mr. & Mrs. McDaniel,

I feel absolutely obligated to respond to the stunning letter I received from you. I must say I was both floored and amazed by the depth of your faith and forgiveness, the latter of which I accept wholeheartedly. The courageousness and compassion you have displayed are virtues I likely will never know, and they speak volumes about your quality as individuals.

Though I fear I will never truly understand the horrible pain I caused you, in recent years, I have tried to imagine my own family living through such a grievous episode, and shudder to think of it. Although they too have suffered considerably from my mistakes, we at least have the luxury of regular correspondence. I am truly blessed to have, as Uriah did, such a loving and supportive family. The knowledge that I took part in destroying something so beautiful has only recently begun to sink in, for I remain, as I have always been, a very selfish person.

Your work with prisoners is inspiring to me, and again testifies to your strength and inherent benevolence. I hope to transform the negative experiences I have created into something positive that may help others someday. To accomplish this, I am intent on educating myself; however, before I can ever be of use to others, I will have to somehow reconcile myself with my past. Your forgiveness is instrumental in this, and you have shown me a capacity for kindness beyond comprehension. The anguish on your faces and the utter despair in your voices on the day of my sentencing will stay with me always; though I tried to put on a tough exterior, I was shaken to the core.

Please, Mr. and Mrs. McDaniel, if a face-to-face visit will in any degree aid you in moving on with your lives, then by all means, please do so. I am currently confined to a super-max facility here at Pelican Bay, and as such am restricted to behind-glass visitations. Perhaps this will be for the better, as it may help alleviate some discomfort and increase our privacy, as opposed to a crowded visiting room. I supplied the warden with the necessary forms, as well as some useful information. I am truly sorry for the damage I have inflicted upon you and your family.

Sincerely,

Joshua Smith

P0222243

Johnny replies, "His letter meant a lot to us, and hearing his remorse for what he had done helped us move forward to setting up a meeting. We began making plans with the prison warden to set up a meeting. Initially, the prison warden was skeptical that our intentions were to 'forgive' the man who had killed our son. In his fifteen-year career as a prison warden, he had never had anyone contact him about coming in to 'forgive' a prisoner. If anything, the prison warden had more worries about someone coming in to 'finish' off the murderer, rather than offer forgiveness. Debbie and I continued to talk to the prison warden, and we spent two months writing letters to obtain special permission for an upcoming visitation with Joshua. The prison warden, as he learned to trust us, finally granted us permission to move forward in scheduling a visitation."

The prison warden had to get additional permission from Joshua, too. If other prisoners learn that victims of the family are visiting an inmate, this can put their life in danger. You see, prisoners have a code that if a fellow inmate gets soft on his victims, he could be killed himself. There is no privacy in the visitation rooms, so there was a risk for him, and we had to be careful about what we talked about. Joshua agreed to go ahead and let us come visit.

In January 2005, we traveled to Pelican Bay State Prison, along with sixteen supporters who prayed for us outside the prison. When we were ready to go in, we all prayed outside, asking God to cover and watch over us. As Debbie and I walked into the prison, we went through two sets of security measures, which included two metal detectors. We told them whom we were there to visit—Joshua Smith—and we were instructed to board a small tram bus.

Joshua was held in a Special Housing Unit (SHU), also known as "the hole." The SHU basically consists of a jail within a prison, or a secured, separate area of the prison, where there are a few halls housing prisoners. These halls are dark and dingy, and each cell consists of a bunk bed, maybe a desk, a toilet/sink combo, a frosted window (so the occupants can't see out of it), and perhaps a shower. This truly is the lowest existence possible in federal prison. The experience of such prisoners is not good. While most prisoners have access to one hour of recreation on weekdays, for some this is too dangerous due to assaults in the recreation cages. Most prisoners instead elect to stay in their cells 24/7.

We traveled ten minutes on the tram through two sections of double-walled concrete and barbed-wire fencing before it stopped in front of a building. We were directed to go through the door in front of us. As we walked in, we saw winged-walls on the left, where prisoners could meet with visitors separated by glass. Johnny thought to himself, *This may not work very well as it will be hard to talk privately.* All of a sudden, a security guard directed us down a hallway and led us into a private, soundproofed room where attorneys met with prisoners. We were so moved that God had surprised us with a private room for meeting Joshua in person. Now we could talk freely.

Friends always ask us, "Didn't you feel nervous going in there?" What I can say is that after eight years, we were ready to take this step and release the stronghold Joshua had on us. So, as we started toward the door, we didn't feel nervous; we felt peace with God and that we could forgive and free ourselves. We slowly opened the door and walked in. We saw him immediately, sitting on the other side of the glass. He was in a white uniform, clean-shaven, with tattoos all the way up his arms. He looked eight years older and far more mature than the young, eighteen-year-old punk we had seen in the courtroom the day he was sentenced.

Debbie reflects, "Amazingly, with the peace of God, all the negative and dark evil vibes that we had experienced over the years were sucked out of the room like a powerful vacuum. All I saw was a young man who was the last person to see Uriah. It was funny how that was so important in my mind. He was the last person to see Uriah. Believe it or not, there was a special bond there, knowing that even though it was an evil act, he was the last person to see Uriah alive. It was a weird bonding; God was with us, and He gave us the strength to love him and forgive him."

Debbie cries, "I will never forget this bonding experience because God filled the room with light, love, and forgiveness. It was something I didn't expect to feel. As I sat down, the presence of God was overwhelming. There was a beautiful, loving, and peaceful white light in the room. I felt completely surrounded by the Holy Spirit's love and protection. Since that time, I have never felt the same strong presence of God . . . it was truly amazing."

Johnny reflects, "We were there to forgive him, and having a private room helped us say what we needed to say. As I looked at him, he looked cleaned up in a white uniform and with many tattoos up and down his arms. The last time I had faced him in court, he was disheveled and in an orange jumpsuit."

As we sat down, one of the first things Joshua said was, "I am not a very emotional person, but I am sorry for what I did. I have no excuses, and I deserve to be in here. My mom quit coming to see me, and that is okay, because I realize I have committed many crimes and she couldn't come and see me anymore. I am supposed to be here because I know I have hurt other people." He went on to say, "When I got your letter, I had to write you back, because I didn't know how you could forgive me and care about my life."

Johnny responded, "I will tell you the truth, Joshua. There was a time when I was so full of hatred and revenge, I could have killed you myself. But deep down, I knew it was not the right thing to do. I learned that God would not forgive me for the things I have done against Him, if I didn't learn to forgive you. For a moment, picture that I have a file folder and when you open it up, it is so full of hatred, suffering, and revenge. It is so full that all the papers are falling out. When I found God, He started taking the hate and revenge out and began filling my folder with love, trust, and forgiveness. This cleaned out my folder of hate, and I learned to love God. I learned that in order to truly forgive you, God has to help me and that I couldn't do it alone.

Johnny continued, "Debbie and I come today with God's love in our hearts to forgive you. God's profound love allows us to be here and actually forgive you in person. God asks everyone to forgive seven times seventy. Never stop forgiving."

Joshua responded, "I will have to check into this God thing. I do read a lot of books."

When we asked him, "How are you doing in here?" he replied with some sadness, "I haven't talked to my mom in two years; it became too hard for her to talk to me, and I understand. I did it to myself. I do a lot of reading and just hanging out in my cell."

Debbie mentions that during the hour and a half they were there, they shared small talk and didn't rehash any of the tragedy. They discussed their prison ministry works, and this gave him hope. He listened intently as we discussed the details of what we covered in the workshops. Debbie said to Joshua, "Our son, Uriah, would want you to have a good life when you get out." He seemed surprised at my statement.

After we all had been talking, it was time to offer him our forgiveness. Johnny asked Joshua to stand up and put his hands on the glass. I put my hands against his on the other side of the glass. He looked down. I said, "Joshua, look into my eyes. I forgive you for murdering my son, and now I want you to forgive yourself." I asked him to repeat these words: "I forgive myself for murdering your son, and I forgive myself for the things I have done against others," then Joshua sat down with his head bowed down. Debbie then got up and asked him to stand and match her hands on the glass. This time he looked into her eyes. She said, "Joshua, with the grace of God, I forgive you for taking Uriah's life, and I hope you can forgive yourself." And then Joshua repeated the words back to Debbie, and they both sat down.

There was a serene silence, and then Johnny asked, "How do you feel now?" We were surprised by his answer and his unusual language. He said, without much emotion and after a long pause, "Well, that was kind of cathartic." I asked him what that meant, and he said, "It means cleansing or crying," and we all started laughing.

Even though Joshua was not emotional during the hour of talking, at the point we stood to leave, he stood up and turned to the side. At the door, we turned back to look at him one more time, and we saw tears streaming down his face. He was touched that we cared about him and had forgiven him. We told him we loved him and that we would be praying for him every day.

Debbie gently reflects, "When we stood to leave, I was surprised that I didn't want to go. Here was one more lost soul who got into trouble because of drugs. It made me feel sad for him. I told him I would pray for him every day. The healing, the forgiveness, and the white light of the Holy Spirit were so intense in the room. I believe the feeling I had will be etched into my mind for the rest of my life. I didn't want to leave that wonderful feeling of peace and comfort. God was with us every step of the way. In fact, if the glass had not been between us, Johnny and I would have both reached out to hug him."

Johnny says, "As we left the prison building, we were overwhelmed by the love of the sixteen friends and supporters who were outside to greet us. It stills makes me cry as I remember hugging and crying with everyone. We thanked God for freeing our hearts. We felt so good. The heavy burden that had been on our hearts for years was lifted. We were FREE at last."

God wants us to forgive so we can be set free. We still have life in front of us. Jesus came that we would all receive Him and live life to the fullest. Forgiveness is essential to any growing, healthy, and lasting relationship. Jesus came to pay the debt of our sin on the cross, making peace for us with the Father. Now the Lord wants us to receive the forgiveness that Jesus purchased on the cross. It is impossible to get to true forgiveness without God. He is the great Healer.

Forgiving the murderer or anyone who has hurt you can only be an act of Jesus' love—it is a sacrificial gift to Jesus. Follow Jesus, and He will lead you through the pain.

Forgiveness is an act of worship. Let go and give it to Jesus. Lay your burdens at the foot of the cross. We have to let go of our pride and turn it over to Him.

One of main reasons He commands us to forgive others is so that we are no longer under the power and injury of the injustice we have experienced. In other words, receiving and giving forgiveness is the way our Lord heals us and brings wholeness back into our lives.

When an injustice is not replaced with forgiveness, the bitterness we hold morphs into worse realities, which affects relationships, marriages, friends, and eventually manifests into stress, rage, illnesses, health concerns, and mental anguish.

Bitterness can cause discouragement, negative thinking, and depression. Such thinking can produce negative thinking errors, such as *I have been injured*, *My life has not turned out as I hoped*, *I will be bitter and be a victim of my circumstances*, and *I will allow my pain to paralyze my life*.

Jesus asked a paralyzed man, "Would you like to get well?" (John 5:6) This may sound odd to us, but the fact remains that there are some people who don't want to change and be healed. By remaining a victim, they give themselves permission to be paralyzed with grief and not move forward to enjoy life. This takes time in the grieving process, and we need God's help to move forward.

As Johnny and Debbie look back at this monumental moment in time forgiving Joshua, they realize God gave them the true gift of forgiveness that is so hard to come by for so many people. God allowed them to give the gift of love and forgiveness to Joshua, the man who had murdered their son, after eight years.

They will remember this moment forever as they continue to cherish the wonderful memories of their son, Uriah. They will never forget what happened, but Johnny and Debbie are now free.

Not Offering Forgiveness	Forgiveness
You owe me.	You owe me for nothing.
I am going to make you pay.	You do not owe me anything.
I am going to recruit other people to hurt you.	I will not even the score.
In the end, I will get my revenge.	I let go, only trusting God.
I will make you regret your actions.	God helps me to forgive you.

[God says,] "Vengeance is Mine, I will repay."

Romans 12:19 NKJV

To forgive is to set a prisoner free and discover that the prisoner was you.

Lewis B. Smedes

Chapter 11

Why, God? Why?

When a child unexpectedly dies, no matter the reason, parents and family members can't help but cry out, "Why, God? Why?" Nothing makes sense as emotions spill over into intense pain, suffering, and endless crying. Nonbelievers may ask, "If God is such a loving and powerful God, why would He allow my innocent child to die?"

Unfortunately, nonbelievers may suffer additional emotional and mental pain as they grieve and mourn, unable to find the peace believers may experience as they grieve. Believers know that God did not "cause" the death to happen, but He does allow events to happen for reasons we won't know until we get to heaven. Believers understand God's purposes are only for good, yet in the middle of our heartache, we may still cry out, "Why, God? Why?" We just don't understand.

Right now, in the middle of your extreme grief, you may not be ready or able to accept the love of Jesus, and that is okay. Just know He loves you and is walking alongside you as He offers you comfort and strength to keep on going each day. You may begin to recognize the love of Jesus through the love of those around you. His love may come through the love of family, friends, neighbors, sympathy cards, emails, flowers, kind words, caring people, therapy, or grief counseling. Jesus' love knows no boundaries.

You may be surprised that even seasoned believers like pastors and ministers, who have been preaching for years and know about Jesus' promises, may still ask the question of "Why, God?"

During the writing of this book, our beloved pastor and his wife lost their young granddaughter to a tragic accident. One day she was enjoying life with her friends, and shockingly, the next day she was gone. There are no adequate words to describe such a heartbreaking loss, and the shock leaves their hearts and the hearts of their family members completely traumatized. Their family is left trying to make sense of this tragedy as they grieve, hurt, cry, and turn to Jesus and each other for comfort.

Our associate pastor, Jeremy, spoke to our congregation the Sunday after the accident, saying, "For me today, it is a sad day. It is a sad day for our pastor's family. It is a sad day for all of us here in the congregation. Do you ever feel like God doesn't answer your desperate prayers? We thank You, God, for helping us with our unbelief. We believe, God, that You are alive and active, yet we wonder if You hear our desperate cries. Do You care? We doubt ourselves as we struggle. We may even feel angry with God for the injustice in the world, especially when the good ones are taken. We don't understand why children's lives are cut short.

"God wants us to speak to Him when we are going through difficult times. He can handle our anger, frustrations, and bitterness." He is a strong

God, who is good, and He can manage those hard, searching questions; especially if we stay in the spirit of Habakkuk 2:1, which reads, "I will climb up to my watchtower and stand at my guardpost. There I will wait to see what the LORD says and how he will answer my complaint."

Our associate pastor went on to say, "Every human emotion is the 'stuff of prayer.' We deal with stuff like joy, hatred, anger, depression, anxiety, and frustrations. God is good, and God modeled for us that whatever we are going though, we should speak to Him. Speak to Him about our disappointments, our struggles, our questions, and concerns.

"When God hears our cries, He may not respond like we expect Him to because God knows what is best for us. God is bigger than us and knows the plans of everyone's lives. For reasons we don't know, He allows us to groan and cry. His silence does not equate to His absence. He is always beside us."

We see in the New Testament, Paul encourages people to bring every concern to God in prayer and enjoy the resulting peace of God, described in Philippians 4:6–7 (NKJV):

Be anxious for nothing, but in everything by prayer and supplication, with thanksgiving, let your requests be made known to God; and the peace of God, which surpasses all understanding, will guard your hearts and minds through Christ Jesus.

Many will ask, "How long? How much longer shall we suffer?" We read in the Scriptures where David prayed to God:

O LORD, how long will you forget me? Forever?

How long will you look the other way?

—Psalm 13:1

Have compassion on me, LORD, for I am weak.

Heal me, LORD, for my bones are in agony.

I am sick at heart.

How long, O LORD, until you restore me?

—Psalm 6:2–3

Three weeks later, our lead pastor and his wife returned home, and on his first Sunday back to church, he quietly shared with an emotional, crackling voice, "Lord, be with us in the middle of this crisis. We don't understand. This is not easy! We worship You. We cry out to You! Father, we look up to You, we praise You, and we lift up Your name. Oh, Lord, we hurt! We give You praise and glory. This is a territory we have not walked through before. Lord, losing a child, so young and innocent, tears us apart. We always believe You know best, yet we have no words. The words don't come to adequately describe how we feel, how we hurt, and how we grieve.

"We have cried so many tears, and through the tears, this is one of the first times in thirty years of ministry when I have asked, 'Why, God?' We know Your words, Lord; we know Your promises; and through our lifetime of learning about You, we know and stand on Your faithfulness as we grieve our loss.

"Lord, I don't have any answers, and I don't understand, but I continue to trust in You. I continue to praise and sing to You. We will not know the 'why' on this side of heaven, but there is one thing I do know this morning, and I believe this with my whole heart as I stand here today.

God is faithful,

God is true,

The Word is true, and

He will be with us until the end."

Our pastor sadly reflected, "In the ICU, when she left to meet Jesus, I leaned down and whispered in her ear, 'I will be with you in a few minutes.' As believers, we know the separation is only temporary, and we will soon be together again. I know in my heart that she is in heaven and all is well and I should rejoice. But the frail, human side of me cries because she is gone and I will deeply miss her. I hurt so much, my strength fails, and my heart aches for my family.

"The shock is difficult to describe. It feels like the time when I fell off a horse, straight onto my back. As I hit the ground, all the air in my lungs was knocked out. I gasped and struggled to breathe, but no air came, my brain was foggy, and then slowly, I felt the air starting to come back into my lungs. That is how it has been for the last few weeks."

During one of the following Sundays, our pastor

once again quietly spoke, "Being a seasoned pastor, this is the first time in my entire life I have asked the question, 'Why, God?' In my eleven years of battling leukemia, I have never asked, 'Why, God?' I just accepted that I had the disease and asked God to lead me through the treatments. Year after year, as I went through those treatments, I never asked, 'Why, God?' But losing someone at such a young age and knowing we won't get to watch her grow up is so heartbreaking. We keep reminding ourselves we will get to see her again soon, and when that day comes, when we are united, the answers will be revealed, and it will be good. Until that time, how do we get through this grief and suffering? We keep worshiping, we keep singing, and we keep on trusting God, over and over. We keep on trusting Him every minute of the day."

The pastor finished his talk with this: "Help us, Lord! We are struggling. My prayer is that everyone will come to know You, Lord. You know it was a true blessing that during a recent church camp, my teenage granddaughter dedicated herself to the Lord to love, praise, and follow Him. After the memorial service, I see young adults holding hands in a circle and praying and giving their lives to You, Lord. Is this what it is all about? One person's life ends to save the lives of others? Does that child inspire others to turn to You, Lord?"

The Scripture says, "And we know that all things work together for good to those who love God, to those who are called according to His purpose" (Romans 8:28 NKJV).

We also know, in Isaiah 55:9: "For just as the heavens are higher than the earth, so my ways are higher than your ways and my thoughts higher than your thoughts."

The strength and power of our pastor's words inspires all of us. Through his grief, we grieve with him and feel the love of Jesus speaking through him. The pastor's message is that no matter what we are going through and no matter how hard it gets, the Lord is with us to give us the strength and comfort we need each minute of the day. The Lord said we would have trials in life—and some trials are harder than others.

Our hearts go out to him as the pastor explains, "Even in the midst of our grief, it is okay to ask why—yet we pray; we hurt—yet we pray; we cry—yet we pray. We pray knowing Jesus is with us. We pray knowing Jesus' ways are right and His ways are good. We draw close to Him as we continue to trust and lean on Him. We turn to family and friends as we express our sorrow and encourage each other to stay close to Jesus."

Our pastor loves to sing one of the old hymns that represents our desire to totally trust in Jesus. It is one of his favorite songs:

'Tis so sweet to trust in Jesus

Just to take Him at His Word

Just to rest upon His promise

Just to know, "Thus saith the Lord."

Jesus, Jesus, how I trust Him

How I've proved Him o'er and o'er

Jesus, Jesus, precious Jesus

Oh, for grace to trust Him more

Pastor states, "The Lord never leaves us if we follow from our hearts and not from our heads. The heart is the seat of our emotions, and through the tough trials, He is there for us. My heart knows I trust Jesus, yet my head goes to 'Why, God?' We need to pray and say the name of Jesus over and over and over to stay in His heart." Pastor ends his sermon with what we read in Scripture: "Trust in the LORD with all your heart, and lean not on your own understanding" (Proverbs 3:5 NKJV).

As families grieve with broken hearts, the Lord knows something we don't know or completely understand. If one family member dies, the grief and love of twenty to forty other family members is an extended release of love for that person and each other. This release of love through grief extends to each other as we cry, comfort, and give words of encouragement. We may continue for years to share our grief and love for our child, extending our love to neighbors, friends, church, and work.

This is Jesus' love. His commandment is to love one another as He has loved us. Believers' souls, when they die, will immediately be in heaven with Christ Jesus. This may result in more family and friends turning to Jesus for their own salvation. The Lord knows who will come to know Him and be with Him for eternity. One person's unfortunate death may result in hundreds to thousands of others being saved.

Dr. David Jeremiah, the pastor of Shadow Mountain Church in California, writes in his bestselling book *God Has Not Forgotten You*: "Perhaps the only thing worse than thinking whether God has forgotten us is the idea that God has forgotten those in our family. Watching our loved ones suffer or try to find their way through trouble may be one of the most difficult things to endure. We want so desperately to help! We want to make things right and we sometimes have difficulty understanding why God doesn't step in to do just that."[17]

Pastor shared on the following Sunday: "As a dad, it has been hard watching my adult son and family hurt as they grieve. I have always been able to offer advice or fix things that needed done. It is what we do as a dad. When my grieving son became quiet, he asked me, 'What do I do, Dad?' I was at a loss for words, and it hurt. All I could say was, 'Honey, I just don't know.'"

Dr. David Jeremiah writes, "God offers us three ways to respond in such moments. You can replace fear with faith, sorrow with God's Word, and your heartache with trust in God."[18]

We may not know the answer right now, yet we have a bit of peace knowing that someday, when we reach heaven ourselves, the answer will be clear, and it will be good. All we can do right now is trust God.

Sadly, while we are in the grieving process, we

need extra help to get us through the sadness, loss, and pain. Dr. Earl McQuay, a minister who lost a son in a tragic car accident, wrote a small book entitled *Beyond Eagles: A Father's Grief and Hope.* In this book, he offered a special note to parents and families who have endured the death of a child.[19] He listed five realities that provided immense comfort to his heart and to his wife's:

The first reality is *Scripture.* The Word of God serves as firm ground as the hurricane of tragedy sweeps over our souls. Scripture, God's promises, truths about heaven and comfort in Scripture, all drew us closer to the Lord.

The second reality is *prayer.* With prayer, you can cry out to the Lord, knowing He sympathizes with you. He answers by giving you the support of others, cards, flowers, or just an encouraging word. In prayer we are able to rest in God's arms, find comfort, and trust Him to turn our heartaches into memories and eventually praise.

The third reality is *friends.* At the time of your greatest need, the members of the body of Christ come to offer comfort. Their prayers encourage us and help us to heal.

The fourth is *memories.* We gave thanks for the years we had with our loved one, remembering the smiles, laughter, adventures, and good times together.

The fifth is *hope.* For the believer, death is not final—only a pause until we can be together again.

In summary, there are not enough comforting words ever to reduce a parent's pain, yet the God we serve and love can give us emotional comfort while we are here on earth. God is everlasting, and He has prepared a place for each of His believers. He has your child in His protection giving them a safe place of love and joy until you see them again. We can give comfort to one another with His Word.

Weeping may endure for a night,
But joy comes in the morning.

Psalm 30:5 NKJV

O LORD my God, I cried out to You,
And You healed me.

Psalm 30:2 NKJV

Chapter 12

Finding Jesus in Your Tears

Jesus knows every tear you have cried; He knows your every thought; and He knows what you are going through in your grief. He loves you more than any person on earth can ever love you. In Scripture, it reads:

You keep track of all my sorrows.

You have collected all my tears in your bottle.

You have recorded each one in your book.

—Psalm 56:8

He has been pursuing you since the day you were born. When you were born, your name was written down in the Book of Life. God even knows how many hairs are on your head. God wants you to talk with Him; He wants a close relationship with you and wants to talk about everything in your life, including the little details.

It is important to come as you are; bring your tears, your sorrow, your depression, and your sinful nature, whether it be alcohol, drugs, infidelity, porn, stealing, hurts, grief, or any other brokenness. Share with Jesus your pain, and share with Him what you need now at this very moment. We are all children of God, and He loves it when we come to Him for healing.

Children are born in the image of God. A child is born through us, not to us. They are born in the image of God with their own spirit when they take their first breath. Scripture says, "So God created human beings in his own image. In the image of God he created them; male and female he created them" (Genesis 1:27). God gifts us with children whom we are to take care of until they return to God's care.

When a child goes to be with the Lord much sooner than we planned, we GRIEVE ... and we don't understand. We cry millions of tears, and our whole life is turned upside down. It is perfectly normal to ask, "Why, God? Why my beautiful daughter? Why my only precious son?" We don't understand, and it may be something we won't know this side of heaven until we get there ourselves. But what we do know is that when we get to heaven, it will be revealed to us, and it will be good. The reason our child died early will be shown to us. We will gently, with love, nod our heads in full approval of God's deep love for us.

Jesus loves you. He loves everyone on earth, more than you can imagine. He has a deep, unconditional love for us. Most of us don't feel worthy of this kind of love, so it can be difficult to accept. We all have some brokenness in our hearts. We may come from walks of life where we were hurt, abused, neglected, rejected, or made to feel unworthy. We need to heal our wounds, and the greatest and only Healer is Jesus. It is not a weakness to seek Jesus; it is the strength of His love for us. As we humble ourselves before the Lord, we break down the barrier that we can do it ourselves without any help.

Jesus knows you. Jesus unconditionally loves each person, and He gives us 'free will' to make the decision to come to know and love Him. He patiently waits, He surprises us with God winks, He heals, He sends friends to help, He protects, and He sends us love.

Jesus is real. He is alive and active in each believer's heart. At this moment, in your pain, you can talk to Him like you would a trusted friend. You don't have to be in church; you don't have to talk to a minister; you don't have to be on your knees; just whisper His name, "Jesus." Say it over and over, "Jesus, Jesus, Jesus." He will hear you.

Jesus hears you. Cry out to Him, and give Him all your hurts. Tell Him what you are going through, and ask for what you need. God is a loving God who knows before you ask, but we have to ask to show that we believe in Him with all our heart, mind, soul, and strength. We have to trust Him. As a loving Father, He may not answer in the manner you want, but He will respond in the manner that is best for you. Remember, the absence of an answer does not mean He is not there. He is always with you.

Jesus is listening. We cry out, "How long shall we suffer?" This expresses the perpetual cry of every human heart who grieves. The cost of losing someone you love results in necessary grief. We wonder if the Lord hears us or even hears the desperation in our prayers. He does hear our prayers. Although we are impatient for God to act, we have to trust that He is at work. Work for good and not for evil.

Jesus is alive. He is at work even if we may not believe He cares. It may be hard to believe God is at work when we experience the injustice of losing a child. Emotions could include great sadness, depression, or even a loss of hope. Losing a child is one of the hardest types of grief to work through, yet God can help, and He will if you give Him a chance.

Jesus is prayer. Pray like you were talking to your best friend. The best prayer language is the words that desperately come out of your mouth, straight from your broken heart. They don't have to be fancy or scriptural from the Bible. The Lord just wants to hear the simple prayers of the brokenhearted in their real words. Above all, give praise to the Lord. He is the Creator of heaven and earth. Let your emotions be known to God, and His peace will come upon you in the most profound way. He desires us to talk to Him. He wants a relationship with you.

Jesus is faith. We dedicate our lives to following Christ Jesus without seeing Him. It's the same as breathing air; we don't see the air, but we have faith that the air is available to breathe. We walk and breathe without questioning. Faith is the same thing; we live our lives trusting that God is there for us. We don't have to see Him; we walk by faith. The Scripture says, "For we walk by faith, not by sight" (2 Corinthians 5:7 NKJV).

Jesus is our Savior. Would you like to invite Jesus into your heart for the very first time? All you have to do is just say these words. Say aloud, "Jesus, I invite You into my heart as my personal Lord and Savior. I believe You are the Son of God and that You died on the cross for my sins. I believe You were resurrected and rose again on the third day. Jesus, I repent of all my sins, and I ask for forgiveness for anything that I have done that hurt You."

Jesus is forgiveness. Ask Jesus to forgive you for any sin you have committed against Him. All humans have sinned because we were born sinners. As stated in the Bible, in Romans 3:23, "For all have sinned and fall short of the glory of God" (NKJV).

If you say these words, believe them with all your heart, and go forth in life to consciously sin no more, you are saved! You are 'born again' as a new believer in Jesus Christ. You give up your old life and become a new person in Jesus Christ. You will spend eternity with Jesus. Eternity is forever!

When we are "born again," we make a decision to give our lives over to God, asking for forgiveness for anything we did that was against God. We agree to follow Jesus and love Him with all of our heart, mind, and soul. He then forgives us, placing a love in our hearts for Him. This allows us to begin "forgiving others" for the sins others have committed against us.

Jesus said to him, "I am the way, the truth, and the life. No one comes to the Father except through Me."

—John 14:6 NKJV

Here are four easy steps to becoming a Christian:

1) Apologize to God for the wrong things you have said, done, or thought toward God and others, and then accept His forgiveness.

2) Believe in Jesus Christ: that Jesus Christ is God's Son, our Savior, whose death on the cross is the key to our victorious life. Ask Him to be a part of your life.

3) Commit yourself to be a follower of Jesus by being guided by Christ's principles and values as you live out your life day by day.

4) Attend a Bible-believing church and begin to learn more about God. Fellowship among believers encourages you to stay in the Word and learn how God wants us to live. This creates a better and more peaceful life.

Remember, the person who killed your loved one likely has severe problems, mental issues, and abuse issues, just like so many lost people. They made a horrible mistake and decided to take an innocent life in a fit of their own anger or as a result of their mental issue. They are in their own torment as they spend years in prison and think about what they have done. If they have a conscience, this will weigh on them for years. If they ask God to forgive them, they will find peace. Remember, we have all have sinned and fallen short of the glory of God. Some people fall further than others, yet the Lord says, "Vengeance is Mine."

It is common for parents who lose a child to want the murderer to "pay." We expect him/her to pay with their life, pay with time in prison, and pay with remorse, but no one can "repay" you for the death of your child. Your child is priceless. Your child is now dancing with Jesus. There is no repayment plan, except through the blood of Jesus.

Remember, Jesus died a horrible death on the cross; He suffered as He took on the sins of the world. After three days, Jesus was resurrected and is alive and lives again.

Forgiveness offers us the same benefit. Your child died at the hands of a murderer. You suffered and take on the sins of the killer, wanting to hurt or kill him to make him suffer, too. When you offer forgiveness, you are 'born again'; you die to self, and you find strength and peace through Jesus Christ. You are resurrected in Him!

Unfortunately, the deep cuts of pain can poison us for life. When we continue to hold on to revenge or pain, we are allowing the killer to have control over our lives, and we stop living. The murderer not only killed our child, but now he or she is slowly killing us and stopping us from living. When we choose to focus our thoughts and anger on the killer, there is no room in our hearts for thoughts or the inner working of God to find healing, joy, or forgiveness. If you come to God and ask for forgiveness for the one who hurt you, you will find an anchor in the Scriptures that is only available to those who know God. True forgiveness recognizes the depravity of evil. We don't ever forget, but we can forgive through God, who will give you the strength. Is it easy? No, but it is rewarding, because you get your life back and help those around you.

You need to always remember that "forgiveness is not being passive about evil. And forgiveness is not brushing off deep hurts as if this didn't happen to you. Forgiveness of this nature is allowing God to handle it and letting Him do the avenging."

Romans 12:19 states, "Dear friends, never take revenge. Leave that to the righteous anger of God. For the Scriptures say, 'I will take revenge; I will pay them back,' says the LORD."

In summary, God intends everything in life for good, even when bad things happen. God is not about any kind of evil; His purposes in life are for good. The good serves and helps others while growing His Kingdom.

We are living in a world where God is in charge and guiding all things for His purpose. If we can truly understand God's heart, we will find a Father who is with us in our pain. We find comfort in knowing that while our world is completely spinning out of control, there is One who upholds all things "by the word of His power" (Hebrews 1:3 NKJV).

How can we forgive others? We can look to the cross, where the world's greatest injustice was committed against the Son of God, Jesus. We can lay our burdens down at the foot of the cross.

Jesus is waiting for you. He is caring for and protecting your child in heaven. You will be with your child again, if you are a believer in Jesus Christ and come to know Him. What a beautiful day that will be . . .

Be still, and know that I am God.

Psalm 46:10 NKJV

Chapter 13

Moving On

In our final interview, Johnny and Debbie McDaniel calmly stated, "After visiting Pelican Bay State Prison to physically forgive Joshua, we had finally reached a new chapter of our lives. We had found freedom in forgiveness, and we had freed ourselves from the prisoner within our souls. We were ready to move on. We think of Uriah every day, but the sting and hurt has subsided, and God had given us the peace that we so desire. After eight long years, we were ready to move out of Oakland, California. We want to leave the big city behind, leave our lives behind, and start life with a new beginning in another state."

We chose a small town close to some special friends. It felt so good to buy a comfortable house on a quiet, residential hillside, and have an environment where we didn't have to worry about big city life. We felt so at peace.

Debbie mentions, "Leaving Oakland with all the friends I had made over the years was hard, yet moving to a smaller town brought peacefulness and a new start on life. We had so many memories with friends. I had been diagnosed with fibromyalgia, and it started getting worse when we moved, and soon I could no longer work. Then, in 2013, I underwent heart surgery for a replacement valve."

Debbie goes on to say, "I will say that when Uriah was killed, I lost my enthusiasm and spark for working. My physical health was affected, and I lost some of my youthfulness in my physical appearance. Stress and grief takes its toll on the human body. On a daily basis, because of fibromyalgia, I lack energy and have a hard time getting out of bed in the morning because of all my nerve pain. Fibromyalgia, even with medication, does not allow me to clean house, cook, or be away from home much anymore."

Johnny adds, "When I decided to retire in 2010, I vowed to take good care of Debbie. I created a beautiful flower garden in our backyard and called it 'Debbie's Park,' so she can sit out there and see the flowers, the green grass, and the trees. It is very private and a heavenly place as we sit on the patio taking in the beauty and quietness. I still think of Debbie as my angel who was there when Uriah and I needed her most . . . and I am most thankful for her coming into our lives. We have been through so much grief and suffering in life, and now the peace of God surrounds us."

I have some buddies I play golf with a couple times a week. I enjoy being out on the greens and seeing how beautiful it is, plus it is so peaceful.

Debbie and I attend church regularly, and I spend one evening a week helping the youth leader of our church with the junior high kids. I love watching the kids with all their enthusiasm for life. The youth are our future, and I enjoy seeing them learn more about Jesus. They will have a better life if they know the Source of all life. I surround myself with dear friends at two weekly Bible studies to continue to learn about my Savior. He is definitely alive, and the Holy Spirit gives me comfort each day.

My commitment to the Lord, Debbie, and Uriah on that tragic day was never to touch alcohol or drugs again, and for twenty-seven years, I have kept that promise. The Lord saved me from a life of destruction, and I am forever grateful. I will never leave Him.

Debbie tenderheartedly explains that "every year in September, I start a countdown of the first ten days of that month, preparing for that September 10th day when we lost Uriah. Johnny and I seem to build up a bit of anxiety as the day approaches.

"When the day arrives, we take quiet time to reflect back on the memories we have with Uriah. We say prayers asking God to watch over us. No, we will never forget our son or any of the wonderful memories we had with him. God helps us through the tough moments and gives us comfort and peace, so we can live life again."

Debbie continues, "Even after twenty-seven years, we still have pictures of Uriah up on the wall, on the living room table, and in a bedroom where we keep our favorite things that represent the wonderful life we had together. I still have some of Uriah's shirts hanging in my closet; they give me such comfort. Every day I think of him and the sweet moments we spent together singing, reading the Bible, or just talking. I say a prayer every day for Joshua, in prison, that his life has changed for the better."

Johnny states, "When I have a down day or things are not going well, I always stop and think of Uriah's smiling face. Yes, I shed a few tears and my heart starts to ache; then I am reminded that because of knowing and believing in Jesus Christ, I will see my son again. This gives me the hope that Jesus promised us, that we will spend eternity together. Sometimes it feels like a long time; so many years have gone by, but the Scripture says, 'A day is like a thousand years to the Lord, and a thousand years is like a day' (2 Peter 3:8–)."

Some people may think that with all the years behind us, we would be 'over' it. When you lose a child, you don't actually get 'over' the loss; you just learn, through Jesus, to walk through it, into acceptance and peace.

We pray every day for Joshua, the murderer, hoping his life has changed for the better and he is making a difference in the lives of other people. We finally released the prisoner inside us, and finding true forgiveness gave us the freedom to live again. We couldn't have done it without the love of Jesus Christ. He is our Savior, our Mighty Counselor, our only Source for the strength to forgive the person who took our son from us.

In summary, as we look back at our lives, we are glad all the big hurdles are behind us. We know, like most people, that we grew up in messy lives, with physical abuse, alcohol abuse, drug addiction, marriage problems, guilt, rage, suicidal ideation, and intense grief. When people look at our lives, they may wonder how we got through it all. The only answer I have for them is "Jesus, Jesus, and more Jesus!" He has saved us in more ways than one. He freed us from bitterness. He gave us the love and freedom to finally heal, forgive, and love again.

At times when we least expect it, Uriah and some memory will come up and gently hit us in the heart. I remind people that "his name IS Uriah,' rather than 'his name WAS Uriah.' He is always with us in our hearts. His favorite number is twenty-two, and throughout life, we laugh when the number comes up, reminding us that Uriah is close by. We can't help but get teary-eyed because that is what we do now. The tears come, but they no longer make us sick inside. We feel the slight pain as we smile gently, knowing that by believing in Jesus, we will get to be with Uriah again. It will be a beautiful reunion of absolute love and peace. We both look forward to that day of seeing our son again. Until then, we will continue to do the Lord's work.

While this book was being written, I found a letter I had written Uriah a few years after he died:

Dear Sweet Uriah,

I love you so much with all my heart and energy. It has been years now since you went to the other side.

I got you a really nice box to put this letter in and decided to leave it on my desk where I can share my joy of sobriety with you. I am so proud of you, Uriah. I just want you to be happy.

I finally bought a beautiful frame that shows the heavenly picture of you holding the cross over us. Thank you so much. What a wonderful gift. I feel your presence all the time. I draw strength from you as you are constantly in my thoughts and heart.

I wish I could talk to you and you were here to talk back to me. I am always wondering what you are doing in heaven. It must be really cool where you are. How are Grandma and Great-Uncle Archie? I love you all so very, very much!

Grandma, please take good care of my boy, and thank you for loving and keeping me safe while you were here on earth.

I miss you, Uriah. I wish we could go swimming together again. I have been trying to play golf as much as I can and am trying to have some fun. Some days it is very hard; other days I do okay.

I am so sorry about what happened to you. I feel so cheated out of our relationship. I know we still have a relationship in our hearts, but not physically seeing you is hard. I hope we did everything you wanted to do. You are loved by so many people. Thank you for your beautiful music and songs. Thank you for being my son, the best son a father could ever dream of having.

I was doing some yard work in the backyard yesterday, and, boy, I sure could have used your help. When I work out in the backyard, I can feel your presence every time. Sometimes I think I even feel you touching me.

I love you, Uriah. I will see you at the beautiful river where we spent so much time. I feel your presence there in the water. You are always in my thoughts and in my heart.

We will someday be together in God's care. God bless you, son!

Thank you for choosing me as your Daddy-O. I love you with all my heart.

Love, Daddy-O!!

A time to weep,

And a time to laugh;

A time to mourn,

And a time to dance.

Ecclesiastes 3:4 NKJV

The Heroes of Forgiveness Honor

International Forgiveness Day

On Sunday, August 1, 2004, Johnny and Debbie McDaniel were honored as "Heroes of Forgiveness" during the 8th Annual International Forgiveness Day Ceremony. They were interviewed on a radio talk show program called *God Talk*, and they shared their story with millions of listeners.

The Worldwide Forgiveness Alliance promotes the first Sunday in August as International Forgiveness Day, hoping to spread awareness about the healing power of forgiveness and to create a "safer, more joyful, and more peaceful world." Robert Plath, an attorney, created "Forgiveness Day" in 1996 to honor the power of forgiveness.

The idea behind Forgiveness Day is to encourage the act of forgiving and seeking forgiveness for past wrongdoings. This serves as a gentle reminder of the healing power of forgiveness and encourages individuals to let go of grudges, resentment, and anger. While it is important to acknowledge that forgiveness is a personal and complex process, the people who manage to walk through the forgiveness process go on to lead more calm and peaceful lives.

Johnny comments, "Forgive others, not because

they deserve forgiveness, but because you deserve peace. You cannot heal unless you forgive and only Jesus can help."

Resources for Assistance

CELEBRATE RECOVERY©

Celebrate Recovery is a safe place to find community and freedom from the painful issues that are controlling our lives. This program is a Christ-centered, twelve-step recovery program for anyone struggling with any kind of hurt, hang-up, or habit that affects their desire to have a better life.

This program started in 1991 at Saddleback Church in Lake Forest, California. John Baker wrote Pastor Rick Warren the "now-famous, concise, 13-page single-spaced" letter outlining the vision God had given John for Celebrate Recovery.

The first night forty-three people attended, and Celebrate Recovery was born. Today, there are now thirty-five thousand churches participating around the world, and that number continues to grow. To date, over five million individuals have completed a Step Study, nine-week study course. This is a program that brings the healing power of Jesus Christ to the hurting and broken through Celebrate Recovery's Step Studies, The Journey Begins, and The Journey Continues.

In addition, Celebrate Recovery is growing in recovery houses, rescue missions, universities, and prisons around the world. This is an exciting and growing outreach opportunity for Celebrate

Recovery. We are a part of something much larger than one church's Celebrate Recovery. We are part of a movement that God is blessing.

The Celebrate Recovery program has about 25 percent alcohol and chemical/drug dependency participants. The other 75 percent have hurts, hang-ups, and habits that may include sexual and physical abuse, mental and emotional abuse, codependency, the death of a loved one(s), the murder of a family member, depression, anxiety, divorce, eating disorders, separation from children, job anxiety, or a medical condition or illness. The list goes on to include any hurt, hang-up, or habit that a person may be suffering from, sometimes in silence, in their life.

Imagine a safe environment where people accept you just the way you are and love you through your pain. The goal is to gently identify the main core issues why you medicate or why you hurt. In doing so, you get down to the root cause of your hurt with the "who, what, why, how it made you react, and the outcome." This helps each person to move through to a point of managing the pain. It can be lifesaving. Jesus Christ is the great Healer.[20]

Life has a way of changing by just a simple phone call in which you hear "that your child died in a car accident"; that "you have terminal cancer"; that "your sister was found murdered"; or that "your husband wants a divorce." All the situations we face in life have an effect on us, some that can change our lifestyles forever. People can harbor bitterness or un-forgiveness for years and not know this is affecting them. They just know they feel angry, depressed, resentful, and unhappy with life.

A dear friend shared her experience with Celebrate Recovery:

Sharon's Testimony

Psalm 6:6 (ERV) says, "Lord, I am so weak. I cried to you all night. My pillow is soaked; my bed is dripping wet from my tears." God is always with us.

I'm a grateful believer in Jesus Christ, I struggle with codependency, and my name is Sharon. My story is one that reflects all of the three Hs of hurts, habits, and hang-ups.

My first five years of life as I remember was filled with love and a great family life. My dad was raised by his Cherokee mother and his Scandinavian father. My grandmother was raised on a Cherokee Indian reservation in Texas; she didn't go to school and was unable to read or write. At some point they moved to California, where they worked in the fields as farm laborers. Their children worked in the fields picking cotton. My dad joined the US Navy at a young age and served four years. He was only home for a short time, when he met my mother and decided to join the US Air Force. He was an airman and refueled planes while inflight. He developed cirrhosis of the liver due to ingesting the toxic fumes. He died at the age thirty, when I was five.

My mother remarried when I was eight years old. I remember being left with many different babysitters throughout the day and night. At the age of nine, I was introduced to their favorite hangout spots and their favorite pool hall. It's strange the things children can remember. I enjoyed going with my parents, as it felt like a playdate because many other children were there. We'd stay in rooms just off the bar; we had everything we needed, including what resembled "healthy" food like chips, soda, and candy. There were lots of games—shuffle board, pinball, and darts—and we got pretty good at those games.

When I was ten, I was blessed with a sister. Debby was born with a cleft lip. Even though she had surgery, her lip didn't heal correctly, and she became self-conscious of her appearance. She was bullied in school because of her appearance, and this led to shyness and low self-esteem. It was difficult for my parents to take a baby to bars, so I was now the babysitter. I would take care of my sister and anything else that needed to be done around the house.

I think this may have been when I developed my codependency, feelings of abandonment, and many hurts. Hurts deal with our heart, emotions, and feelings. A counselor once said that our emotions won't last forever, but they will wait forever. All these emotions were buried for many years.

When I was thirteen, I met a boy who was sixteen; he was at our house often, even when my parents were not home. Guess what happens to unsupervised children? I was lonely and starved for affection. I became pregnant, and we married and I'd had a baby—all by the age of sixteen. I quit school my sophomore year of high school and moved into my own house. But there was still the matter of my sister. I took care of her while my mother worked and on the evenings when they didn't pick her up. And the cycle continued.

After my son was born, I attended night school and received my high school diploma within two years. When I turned eighteen, I applied for a job, and to my surprise, I was hired. My parents had to now be responsible for my sister. I attended college at night, worked a full-time job, and managed to care for my son. My daughter was born four years later. I moved up the corporate ladder rapidly. After thirteen years of marriage, my husband and I divorced. I became very bitter and full of anger and resentment.

Fast-forward a few years, to when my mother and stepdad retired and decided to do something different and pursue their love—they bought a bar. That's exactly the type of business that an alcoholic should own. My sister worked for them. Within a few years, my mother was diagnosed with lung cancer, and within two years the cancer had spread to her brain. She had many bouts of cancer treatments and was continually sick. I now had to help with the bookkeeping for their household and business while working and taking care of my own children. And, on occasion, I worked in their bar.

This is another codependency lesson, with control and lots of responsibilities. I never learned to say the word "no." If anything needed to be done, I could do it. I'm not saying that this is a bad trait; however, I didn't know the meaning of boundaries. I never wanted my family to suffer any consequences, so if I had the ability to provide a soft landing, I would take on their responsibilities and hardships.

My sister had her own struggle with drugs and alcohol. As a teenager she surrounded herself with people who gave her attention and "love." She certainly didn't get it at home. I could totally relate to that; my parents never did see how their reckless behavior affected their children.

My sister married an older man, and he took her down a dark path of drug abuse and criminal activity. They gained unauthorized access to my parents' ATM card and were stealing three hundred dollars per day. I convinced my mother to report the card stolen to the bank. They were later arrested and convicted for that theft. Debby was sentenced to nine months in jail, and her husband received three years in prison due to his prior convictions. This turned out to be a major turning point in my sister's life. Once she was released from jail, she stayed clean and sober. My sister divorced her husband and moved on with her life. She called me one day and said her ex-husband was being released from prison. I asked her, "How do you feel about him being released?" She said it wasn't a problem; she had moved on. She had, but he hadn't. I received a call a few days later from my dad, and I could hear my mother crying in the background. He said he had found my sister dead in her apartment. I dropped to my knees at that instant—the pain was unbearable. Her ex-husband had killed her.

My mother was heartbroken and died three months later from brain cancer. During those final three months of her illness, she apologized for all the pain that she had caused us; we were close during this difficult time. One day I walked into her hospital room to find she was in a coma, but with her eyes closed, she was reciting the Lord's Prayer. The same week my mom died, my sister's killer was scheduled to go to trial. He accepted a plea bargain and received twelve to twenty-four years in prison.

During this time, I was dating Hank, my future husband. He walked beside me during this tragedy. We've since been married for thirty-five years. In October 1990, we received a call that my husband's son, Brian, had been in an accident and was in the hospital. We walked into the hospital room and found Brian connected to numerous machines. As a trained EMT, Hank knew what was happening. This healthy twenty-two-year old man now had no brain activity. The decision was made the following day to remove Brian from life support. We found out that there had been a confrontation between Brian and another man. This man had pushed Brian down a set of stairs and then kicked him in the head.

Two weeks later, my precious grandmother drove herself to the Kern River, walked down an embankment, and into the river. Her body was found two days later. How on earth an eighty-three-year old woman could walk down that embankment was beyond my understanding. But she was definitely determined. What would cause this beautiful Christian woman to commit suicide? I did find a prescription for sleep medication for her with a warning that said, "This drug could cause suicidal tendencies." Was this the cause? I don't know.

The man who killed my stepson was arrested, but the district attorney decided against prosecution due to lack of evidence. My husband was trying to deal with his grief, but that grief turned into rage and anger. He found comfort in alcohol. For years he couldn't even mention Brian's name without tears. Later he didn't mention him at all; it was safer that way. My mother-in-law was then diagnosed with cancer and passed away two years after Brian.

During this time, my son became involved heavily with drugs. We spent many sleepless nights not knowing where he was. He'd be gone for days; we'd drive around looking for him for hours. Many times, we'd find him under bridges, hiding in bushes or in different hotel rooms. On at least three different occasions, we were called to the hospital because he'd had a drug overdose. It is a miracle he didn't die. No matter how hard we tried to help him nothing seemed to work. He tried different drug rehabs without success. On one occasion, he went to Teen Challenge; we were invited to a chapel service, and this had a major impact on my husband. Watching these young men struggling with addiction really touched his heart. Hank was fifty years old when he gave his heart to the Lord in that chapel service, and he decided to let go of the revenge and rage that had overtaken his heart.

In 2002, I started to have breathing problems; I was diagnosed with a disease called tracheal stenosis. The only doctor close enough to help me was at UCLA Medical Center. I had reconstruction surgery on my trachea, and I was in the hospital for seventeen days. I had a tracheotomy with a t-tube in my throat, and it took a year for me to have the tracheotomy closed. Ninety-five percent of people with tracheal stenosis have their tracheotomies for life, and they rarely return to full use of their voice. I was in the telecommunications business and responsible for the entire region for a large corporation. Without a voice, I couldn't be effective, and so I decided to retire. We had already relocated to Oregon and were making the monthly doctor visits to California. My voice came back slowly, and I can now speak.

When we first moved to Oregon, we didn't attend church; it was too difficult for me to function away from home. I had to use a suction machine several times a day. That year was a very humbling experience, and it gave me a new appreciation for people with various disabilities.

In 2002, we found our way to a wonderful church close to where we lived. In 2007, I was talking to our pastor about a recovery program, and after some research a program called Celebrate Recovery was found. The program was ordered, and I was asked if I'd be willing to help. I said sure, I was willing to help people with drug and alcohol problems. After all, I knew all about dealing with those people. I'd been dealing with that type of dysfunction my entire life. Wow, was I wrong—it wasn't just about drugs and alcohol; there was something I could actually learn. Hmm, I think that's called DENIAL.

I read lesson one on denial, and on the first page it said, "There are two things I would like to point out. First, God has a particular race and a unique plan, for each of us. He has a plan for good, not a life full of dependencies, addictions, and obsessions."

The second thing is that we need to be willing to get rid of all the unnecessary baggage, the past failures, in our lives that keep us stuck. "Let us strip off anything that slows us down or holds us back, and especially those sins that wrap themselves so tightly around our feet and trip us up. Many of us are stuck in bitterness over what someone has done to us. We continue to hold on to the hurt and we refuse to forgive the ones who have hurt us. But holding on to that hurt and not being willing to forgive the person, who hurt us in the past, is allowing them to continue to hurt us today, in the present. Working this Christ-centered recovery program will, with God's power, allow us to find the courage and strength to forgive them." Wow, I thought I was going to help someone else, and then I realized that I myself had a lot of baggage.

I recently learned that a hang-up is our belief system and the way we think of ourselves. They drive our habits. Codependency can be a habit. We are hindered if we don't address our hurts and hang-ups. Did you know that a habit is an outward symptom of inward pain? Childhood hurt is the root of codependency. Wounds of trauma are not always visible, but the effects are.

I found out that that my sister's ex-husband died in prison. I Googled his name, and there he was, one of the first patients in his prison to receive hospice care. The article stated that he had committed a murder; it didn't give any details. But there was an interesting footnote that stated that he had become a Christian while in prison. I was angry about that. I then had a real-life experience with the Lord. He spoke these words to my heart: *Sharon, you're always so happy when someone from Celebrate Recovery accepts Me, but not when he did.* That's called 'conviction.' I realized I had not forgiven him for killing my sister.

How many times had I taught on forgiveness, and yet I hadn't been able to offer forgiveness myself. I have a new understanding of forgiveness. I held on to unforgiveness and bitterness all those years. I had to make amends to the Lord and ask God for forgiveness through the power of Jesus, and with the tools we learn at Celebrate Recovery, we can be freed from the bondage of any sin.

People think Christians are bound by the chains and rules of the Bible, when in reality the world is bound through their hurts, habits, and hang-ups. We've been set free to pursue the best we can be through the Lord. In 2017, I moved my stepdad into an assisted living facility. When I was unpacking boxes, I found a card my sister wrote to her dad from jail thirty-five years ago. She wrote about David in the book Psalms, and a quote about the Lord that stated, "Without You I was nothing, I could not do what was right. So, stay with me, abide in me, and help me with the fight." She wrote, "I love you, Dad, with all my heart, don't ever doubt that. Thank you for everything you've ever done for me. I'll try to make it all up to you. I love you, Love, Deb."

God is so faithful; He waited all those years to reveal to me that my sister was truly saved. But I had to forgive before I was ready to receive His gift. God is never late. "I will lead the blind by ways they have not known, along unfamiliar paths I will guide them; I will turn the darkness into light before them and make the rough places smooth" (Isaiah 42:16 NIV).

My son still struggles with drugs, and two years ago we found him trying to stay warm in a dumpster. He begged for help, and we found a program in the city where he lives. After eight months, though, he walked away. He again later called and begged for help. As a codependent, remember I am "the fixer" for my family. I felt the Lord say, *You're getting in My way.* I then said, "No, son, I can't help you this time. You'll have to rely on the Lord." He was so angry with me, but he found a sober living home. I wanted to fix him, and I can't, but God can. To date he has a job and a place to live. I continue to pray daily for his continued sobriety.

In Genesis 9:13 it says, "I have placed my rainbow in the clouds. It is the sign of my covenant with you and with all the earth." So, what if I stopped naming my storms and started naming my rainbows instead? Within God's promise is also a reminder that the storms of life do not have the power to destroy us. They may cause damage, but even in their destruction, they leave room for Jesus to step in and provide, teach, comfort, and save. If I stay focused on Him, I will always find rainbows at the end of my storms.

Presently, I have a great husband, three grandsons, a new granddaughter-in-love, and a beautiful daughter who all bring me joy, and I'm going to have a great-granddaughter soon.

The steps at Celebrate Recovery work no matter what the struggles are—divorce, death, addiction or hurts of any kind. It all starts with the first step: to admit. And admitting may just mean in your denial admitting that you need God. And I guarantee that God will never waste a hurt. Thank you for letting me share my story.

If you find yourself in a place of hurts, hang-ups, and habits that are making your life unmanageable, contact the nearest Celebrate Recovery group or go online to www.celebraterecovery.com for more information. Once you ask Christ into your heart as your Lord and Savior, true healing and recovery can begin.

Help is available today: 1-800-273-8255

Emergency 911

Suicide & Crisis Lifeline 988

Website: http://www.celebraterecovery.com

The National Organization of Parents of Murdered Children

Website: pomc.org

Email: natlpomc@pomc.org

Phone: 513/721-5683

Fax: 513/345-4489

The largest impact of a death of a loved one by homicide is on the survivors. The families and friends who suffer the pain and anguish of knowing their loved one died at the hands of another individual is compounded with so many complicated issues. Families working through these issues deserve absolute compassion and a caring heart from everyone they encounter as they grieve.

When a child, spouse, sibling, or loved one dies by homicide, there can be many unique issues that may complicate the grieving process for the parents and family members left behind. The child's body may be the only evidence, and an autopsy and investigation may cause a lengthy delay in the release of the body for burial. Authorities may need to interview parents and other family members looking for suspects, creating a re-victimization of those survivors who are in the most acute pain. A police investigation can take weeks, months, and even years. Further complications arise because the family wants quick justice for their child, perhaps even stopping their own grieving process. Police need to find the suspect; there is a trial and sentencing, which may take years and years.

Over time, the child may become dehumanized by the police, the press, and the prosecutors as they refer to the child as a "victim," "the body," and/or "the deceased." If someone is charged with the murder, there is a trial, and possible appeals, which can take years. People may cast blame on the child for being in the "wrong place" or "behaving in a way that may have contributed to the murder."

Parents and families can feel like they are living in a nightmare. Murder is a violation of fairness in the right to live a just life. As time passes, families may feel intense reactions of rage, revenge, anxiety, depression, hopelessness, and an inability to sleep or eat. Other reactions may include fear, frustration, survivor's guilt, and self-blame for not being able to protect their child. All these reactions are normal and need to be addressed in the grieving process.

According to the Parents of Murdered Children (POMC), the death of a loved one, especially an innocent child, leaves the survivors with problems that can seem insurmountable. These problems may include:[21]

- Isolation and helplessness in a world that is seen as hostile, uncaring, and frequently blaming of the victim.

- Feelings of guilt for not having protected the victim. Fathers bear an unnecessary burden in our society, believing in their soul that their special role is one of protector. They suffer in silence with this pain.

- The memory of a mutilated body at the morgue: "How much did my loved one suffer?"

- Getting back the personal belongings of a murder victim.

- Sensational and/or inaccurate news media coverage.

- Lack of information about what killed your loved one.

- Endless feelings of grief.

- Loss of ability to function on the job, at home, or in school, etc.

- The strain on marriages and family relationships.

- Effects on health, faith, and values.

- Effects on other family members, children, friends, co-workers, etc.

- Indifference of the community, including professionals, to the plight of survivors.

- Society's attitude regarding murder as a form of entertainment.

- Financial burden for medical and funeral expenses.

- Medical expenses for stress-related illnesses and professional counseling for surviving families.

- Financial burden of hiring private investigators, etc.

- Public sympathy for murderers.

- The feeling that the murderer, if found, gets all the help; survivors of homicide victims have few rights.

- Outrage about the leniency of the murderer's sentence.

- Disparities in the judicial system. Frequently punishments for stealing property can be greater than for someone who takes a life.

- Anger over a plea-bargain agreement.

- Frustration of not being allowed inside the courtroom during the trial.

- Unanswered questions of "What happened?"

- Delays in the trial, appeals, etc.

- Bitterness and loss of faith in the American criminal justice system.

- Constantly reliving your story through the dreaded parole process.

As you can see from this list, the problems of survivors can seem endless. It is important to get as much help as you can to maneuver through the system as you grieve your loss. You can't do it alone. Stand with others who have suffered a loss, too. The website of Parents of Murdered Children has a wealth of information that can assist you.

Contact the National Organization of Parents of Murdered Children for the help you need to maneuver through the justice system as you grieve the loss of your child.[21]

The Compassionate Friends

Today TCF has over six hundred chapters serving all fifty states plus Washington D.C., Puerto Rico, and Guam, that offer friendship, understanding, and hope to bereaved parents, siblings, grandparents, and other family members during the natural grieving process after a child has died. Around the world, more than thirty countries have a Compassionate Friends presence, encircling the globe with support so desperately needed when the worst has happened.

You Are Not Alone

When your child has died, suddenly it seems like all meaning has been drained from your life. When you wake in the morning, it's difficult to get out of bed, much less live a "normal" life. All that was right with the world now seems wrong, and you're wondering when, or if, you'll ever feel better.

We've been there ourselves and understand some of the pain you are feeling right now. We are truly glad that you have found us but profoundly saddened by the reason. We know that you are trying to find your way in a bewildering experience for which no one can truly be prepared.

When you're newly bereaved, suddenly you find yourself on an emotional roller coaster where you have no idea what to expect next. Whether you are parents, grandparents, siblings, or family members, we hope you find some information here that might be helpful to you during this difficult time.

TCF MISSION STATEMENT

The mission of the Compassionate Friends: When a child dies, at any age, the family suffers intense pain and may feel hopeless and isolated. The Compassionate Friends provides highly personal comfort, hope, and support to every family experiencing the death of a son or a daughter, a brother or a sister, or a grandchild, and helps others better assist the grieving family.

The Compassionate Friends was founded over fifty years ago when a chaplain at the Warwickshire Hospital in England brought together two sets of grieving parents and realized that the support they gave each other was better than anything he, as a chaplain, could ever say or provide. Meeting around a kitchen table, the Lawleys and the Hendersons were joined by a bereaved mother and the chaplain, Simon Stephens, and the Society of the Compassionate Friends was born. The Compassionate Friends jumped across the ocean and was established in the United States and incorporated in 1978 in Illinois.

Each chapter, along with the supporting National Office, is committed to helping every bereaved parent, sibling, or grandparent who may walk through our doors or contact us.[22]

©2016 The Compassionate Friends

Contact Information

National Office

Address:

The Compassionate Friends
48660 Pontiac Trail
#930808
Wixom, MI 48393

(877) 969-0010

https://www.compassionatefriends.org

What Is Alcoholics Anonymous?

Alcoholics Anonymous is a fellowship of people who come together to solve their drinking problem. It doesn't cost anything to attend AA meetings. There are no age or education requirements to participate. Membership is open to anyone who wants to do something about their drinking problem.

AA's primary purpose is to help alcoholics to achieve sobriety.

For more information in finding an AA meeting near you, contact: https://www.aa.org/what-is-aa

What Is Narcotics Anonymous?

NA is a nonprofit fellowship or society of men and women for whom drugs had become a major problem. We are recovering addicts who meet regularly to help each other stay clean. This is a program of complete abstinence from all drugs. There is only one requirement for membership, the desire to stop using.

For more information on finding a NA meeting near you, contact: https://na.org/

Suicide Prevention Hotline 988

In 2020, Congress designated the new 988 dialing code to be operated through the existing National Suicide Prevention Lifeline. SAMHSA sees 988 as a first step toward a transformed crisis care system in America.[23]

For more information, go to: https://www.samhsa. gov/find-help/988

Afterword

God nudged me with the idea to write another book while attending a silent retreat for three days. Even though I had passion to write about prophecy again, God guided me in another direction. Johnny McDaniel had started attending our home Bible study. After a few weeks, he brought in a copy of the letter he and his wife had written to the man who had killed their son. He gave me a copy, and the next night, when I read the letter, I couldn't believe what I was reading. I found myself crying, thinking that this is how God wants us to forgive everyone for everything. As the tears kept falling, I read it again. God revealed to me in that moment: *This is true forgiveness—write about this.*

Eight months later, after more than forty hours of interviews, this book, *Forgiving the Killer While Grieving Uriah*, was born. Johnny and Debbie McDaniel opened up their lives and their hearts to me as they relived and retold their story. As we talked, God led us through grief, anger, resentment, healing, and finally, forgiveness. I watched them heal wounds that had been left unopened for years. We will always be close friends because of the road we traveled together.

Each evening before I sat down to write, with piles of notes in front of me, I asked God to give me the words for this book. His words to me were: *Susan, you are enough as you are because I made you in My image. I*

am using you as a vessel to write these words for this book.
Here is where you belong—to write for the glory of God.
Do not be anxious, but instead pray and be thankful for all
I have done.

Thank You, God . . . for Your words!

Notes

1. Bill Dunn & Kathy Leonard, *Through a Season of Grief* (Nashville: Thomas Nelson).

2. Parents of Murdered Children website: http://pomc.org.

3. Ibid.

4. Child Find of America, Website, Facts & Stats on Missing Children: http://childfindofamerica.org.

5. National Vital Statistics System—Mortality Data.

6. Narcotics Anonymous, What is NA?: https://na.org/.

7. Alcoholic Anonymous, What is AA?: https://www.aa.org/what-is-aa.

8. Edgar A. Guest, "A Child Loaned," http://www.familyfriendpoems.com/poem/a-child-of-mine-by-edgar-albert-guest.

9. Susan Brunton, "Purple Orbs," https://www.spiritualunite.com/articles/purple-orb-meaning/.

10. Elisabeth Kübler-Ross, *On Death and Dying* (1969), https://www.psycom.net/stages-of-grief.

11. Robert Enright, University of Washington, Educational Psychology, MensHealth.com.

12. Robert Morgan, "God Works All Things Together for Your Good" (2020).

13. Benny Hinn website: http://www.bennyhinn.org.

14. Jennifer Allwood, "Get Unstuck and Stay Unstuck."

15. Pelican Bay State Prison: https://en.wikipedia.org/wiki/Pelican_Bay_State_Prison.

16. Ibid.

17. Dr. David Jeremiah, "God Has Not Forgotten You" (Nashville: Thomas Nelson, 2021), 68–70.

18. Ibid., 75–76.

19. Ibid.

20. Celebrate Recovery, "What Is Celebrate Recovery?" https://www.celebraterecovery.com/.

21. Parents of Murdered Children: http://natlpomc@pomc.org.

22. Compassionate Friends: https://www.compassionatefriends.org.

23. Suicide Prevention, Call 988: https://www.samhsa.gov/find-help/988.

About the Author

Susan Free has spent thirty-two years teaching classes on psychology, relationships, and various Bible studies, primarily in women's ministries. She has also taught community education classes at Portland Community College in subjects regarding psychology and real estate. In the past, she also served as a grief and stepfamily counselor.

Her first book, *Ready or Not: The Lord Is Coming* (2015), is available online through Amazon and Barnes & Noble.

A native Oregonian, Susan enjoys writing, teaching, hiking in the Cascade Mountains, camping, and spending time with family and friends. She and her husband, Robert, have four daughters and four grandchildren and enjoy a quiet life in Redmond, Oregon.

Susan received a Bachelor of Arts degree in psychology/social science from Marylhurst University in West Linn, Oregon.

For more information about ordering additional books or reading blogs on grief and forgiveness, visit our website at: http://freetheheartministries.com. If you have any questions or would like to contact the author, please email: freetheheartministries@gmail.com.